THE POLITICS

This book is a stimulating, vigorous study of   ool
system by an eminent Canadian political scientist and edu.   Dr.
Frank MacKinnon examines the roles of politicians, officials,
trustees, and others who today wield the power in education, and
discusses the effect of their administration on the schools, the
teachers, and the curriculum.

Dr. MacKinnon advocates strongly taking the politics out of
education, and delegating more responsibility and freedom to the
schools and to the teachers. Only by this means, he feels, can
education become sufficiently effective in a democratic society and
in a challenging and uncertain world. The kind of changes to the
administration of schools and in the status and functions of teachers
required to bring about improvement have long since been made,
Dr MacKinnon holds, in other governmental activities and in other
professions. The changes he recommends will, he suggests, provide
better educational facilities for the country as a whole and better
schooling for a larger number of children.

Dr. MacKinnon has taught in both high school and university,
and, as principal, he has administered every level from grade one to
the second year of university including normal school. He has thus
dealt with pupils of all ages and experienced a wide range of
educational administration. He has served on many educational
boards and committees. From this extensive background he draws
many telling examples and anecdotes that will strike home. His
comments and suggestions, made to provoke discussion and
encourage improvement, will be of interest to members of
provincial and municipal governments, school boards,
administrators and teachers, and all citizens concerned about the
education of young people.

Although Dr. MacKinnon hits hard he does so not just to break
down existing institutions, but because he has strong faith in the
capacities of children and teachers. He covets for the latter a place of
dignity and respect, and for the former an opportunity to develop
individual character and initiative. He is, in fact, a believer in
education.

DR. FRANK MACKINNON (1919-2006) was an eminent Canadian political scientist and educator. He was educated at Prince of Wales College, McGill University, and University of Toronto (Ph.D., 1950). After serving in the Department of Political Science at Carleton University, Dr. MacKinnon became Principal of Prince of Wales College in Charlottetown, Prince Edward Island until 1968. He then joined the Political Science Department at the University of Calgary until his retirement in 1984.

THE POLITICS
OF EDUCATION

A Study of the Political
Administration
of the Public Schools

FRANK MacKINNON

UNIVERSITY OF TORONTO PRESS

TO PHILIP, DAVID, PETER,
AND PAMELA

Preface

I HAVE LONG OBSERVED THAT EVERY PHASE OF EDUCATION IS AFFECTED by politics and that the virtues of government control are taken for granted in the school system to an extent impossible in any other activity in the state. The limitations of this control, however, I have found widely known but rarely discussed out loud. My studies and experience in both political science and education led me to wonder how this unusual situation can be consistent with the generally accepted principles of parliamentary government and public administration and with the management of such important institutions as schools. For the last eight years, therefore, I have explored the subject through extensive reading and discussions with many people during visits to every province in Canada and abroad. This book is the result. It is offered as a constructive, though necessarily critical, approach to educational administration and as an indication of the kind of reform the school system badly needs.

My acknowledgments are so numerous that it is impossible to name everyone who has helped. I have sought opinions and information from many teachers and officials and I thank them all most warmly. I am deeply grateful to the Nuffield Foundation which made it possible for me to explore this subject in Britain and to the British Council which arranged visits to many schools and colleges there.

I have had several welcome opportunities of getting opinions on the ideas expressed in this book from senior educational authorities. I gave parts of the material in chapters II and III in the form of papers to the Canadian Conference of Deans and Professors of Education in Montreal and to the Atlantic Provinces Central Advisory Committee on Education in Wolfville. I made a few general observations on the subject in an essay in J. Katz (ed.), *Canadian Education Today* (McGraw-Hill, 1956). The resulting discussions were most informative and encouraging. I also tested the first draft of the book by sending it to five well known authorities in different parts of Canada: three heads of university departments of "education," a former minister of education, and an officer of the Canadian Teachers' Federation who is also a school principal. From them I received many helpful observations and suggestions and I thank them warmly.

I am especially grateful to Miss Francess Halpenny, Editor of the University of Toronto Press, and her staff for much valuable advice and assistance in preparing the manuscript for publication. Above all, my wife has helped with encouragement and patience at every stage of the work.

F.M.

Prince of Wales College
Charlottetown

Contents

THE POLITICS OF EDUCATION

1. Introduction

TELLING OTHER PEOPLE WHAT TO DO HAS ALWAYS BEEN ONE OF THE most popular, and yet most difficult, arts of man. People are more inclined to instruct and command others than to mind their own business; and their willingness to do what they in turn are told has rarely matched the eagerness of others to advise them. The educational system is the largest instrument in the modern state for telling people what to do. It enrolls five-year olds and tries to direct their mental, and much of their physical, social, and moral development for twelve or more of the most formative years of their lives. The enormous importance of this system is obvious. What is not so obvious is the fact that the state, just like individuals, finds irresistible the natural tendency to instruct and command, while, on their part, young scholars have an equally natural tendency to resist instruction, even from so august a sponsor as the state. The meeting of these two tendencies is the cause of what is currently called the "crisis" in public education.

The very titles of recent studies by eminent educationists indicate an emergency: *The Exploding World of Education, Educational Wastelands, Crowd Culture, So Little for the Mind,* and *Quackery in the Public Schools.* Yet the comments on these works by other educationists indicate a wide divergence of opinion on the facts of the situation. Seldom has there been so much controversy. Rarely, too, has so much depended on the outcome of the issue, for democracy itself is on trial and its strength depends greatly on that of its foundation-stone—education.

The controversy is as much political as pedagogical. Methods of teaching are involved, of course, but the inescapable fact is that the state is now so involved in every phase of education that education is a political activity, and its problems are, to a large extent, problems in governmental administration. Therefore those who examine weaknesses in the school system should take a look, not only at the schools, the teachers, the pupils, and the curriculum, but also at the politicians and the pressure groups, the civil servants, and the trustees concerned with education. May there not be "wastelands" in politics too? The term "crowd culture" can surely be applied to public opinion sometimes; and "quackery" is just as possible in departments of education as it is in the schools.

The crisis today is particularly lively because the state, being completely in control, is doing an abnormal amount of telling, not only to young scholars, but to schools and teachers as well. For the children it provides an official programme of studies with official texts, official examinations, and official certificates, all carefully arranged and "authorized" by official regulations and instructions. To the schools the state gives no power of their own; and the teaching profession is a kind of low-drawer civil service, trained, licensed, hired, inspected, and directed by the state. No other activity, institution, or profession is in this extraordinary position; education in North America is now the most completely socialized activity in modern society.

State participation in education meets an obvious need. For centuries schools were managed by individuals, churches, and other groups. Eventually the idea developed of minimum educational opportunities for all children, regardless of circumstances or location, and the provision of education then passed to the state as the only authority capable of serving the whole community. Soon there were added to this responsibility powers of compelling attendance, laying down the curricula, employing teachers, and enforcing rules and regulations. Many other functions, formerly exercised by the family, home, church, and employer, were also turned over, either because the state wanted them, or because these bodies were unable or unwilling to handle them.

The amount of power over the minds of thousands of children, over many schools, and over the determination of vital social policy, is thus simply enormous. Now it is only logical that in a democracy this power should be made responsible to the elected representatives of the people. It is too dangerous to leave it unattended lest it get into the wrong hands. Totalitarian organizations of many kinds have all too readily secured power by gaining control of an educational system and indoctrinating the children for the sake of their own power. Consequently, the state as the responsible servant of the people is the safest master of their educational system.

State education, however, cannot be infallible because there is nothing infallible about the officials in central, local, or municipal governments. Just because these officials are elected and because they wield power does not necessarily mean that in their hands education is safe and good. There is nothing infallible about public opinion either; just because it is given free scope in education does not mean that the public interest is automatically served, for misguided and selfish motives have as much scope as desirable ones, and even the best ones are often in conflict. Education is put into public hands for safety's sake; its efficiency must still depend largely on the skill of those hands. "Experience," said Thomas Arnold, "seems to point out no one plan of education as decidedly the best; it only says, I think, that public education is the best when it succeeds. There is much chance about it."[1]

One must ask if the element of chance is, in fact, too great in the systems of public education in North America. Are there adequate compensations for the excesses and mistakes of state control and the aberrations of public opinion? Investigation leads one to wonder. Other activities in society are not so unguarded. In government itself there is a "loyal opposition" to check the cabinet, a judiciary with freedom from political interference, and an elaborate election

[1]Norman Wymer, *Dr. Arnold of Rugby* (London: Hale, 1953), pp. 139–40.

procedure to prevent malpractice in the choice of legislators. Most institutions and professions which serve the public are able to do so largely on their own terms and with some protection from political interference. The ancient principle that democracy works best when it is not carried to excess is still recognized in most fields. Is it in education?

This question is imperative. Education is particularly vulnerable to certain characteristics of mass politics and urgently needs compensation for them. Popular support, for example, is fickle; fashion (which is not public opinion) changes rapidly; and people will often agree *en masse* to what they would never approve as individuals. In trying to please everybody, it is easy to please nobody. Everybody's business can become nobody's responsibility. What is required to meet these peculiarities is, of course, leadership, which is difficult to ensure in a field where responsibility rests on no one in particular.

Another characteristic of mass politics, and a dangerous one, is the readiness with which certain people will attempt to divert education from its real purpose, which is to sharpen the minds and increase the abilities of young people, and use it to control minds and direct abilities. The school system is vulnerable to pressure, propaganda, and indoctrination which, with various groups and in different places, can be interpreted as "good" and "bad." It is too easy for minds to be controlled and opinions standardized in these days of mass communication by press, radio, and television, mass rivalry of nations, religious denominations, and political parties, and mass recreation provided by spectator sports. Education is safe so long as the freedom of individual development for the individual's sake is encouraged. And democracy is strong so long as it is based on a thinking, well-informed people. But the moment education is allowed to become mere control on the part of those wanting to manipulate minds and abilities for their own ends, the school becomes just a prefabricated opinion factory in which individualism is discounted and feared. "The organized political, social, and religious associations of our time," warns Albert Schweitzer, "are at work to induce the individual man not to arrive at his own convictions by his own thinking, but to make his own such convictions as they keep ready made for him."[2] If this can be said of schools, they are neither educational nor democratic, and some safeguard must be provided to enable them to discharge their real responsibilities.

The natural resistance to education mentioned earlier also requires compensation. In one way resistance is fortunate and should be cultivated, for without it ideas would be accepted indiscriminately. Yet in another way resistance may be mere perversity; people often won't do what is good for them, and they often like to do something just because someone tells them not to do it. Education, therefore, may not always be regarded as a "good thing." It is invariably subjected to a peculiar mixture of enthusiasm and opposition from those who come in contact with it. It can command hard work and loyal support: it can provoke laziness, suspicion, and hostility. It can be exhilarating because the search for truth can bring much satisfaction: it can be discouraging because the truth is hard to define and, even when it is apparent, people often reject it. Indeed truth is particularly evasive where zealous control, which many people think essential to education, is too great. All the main advances in education have had to overcome zealous control and resistance to truth, and no system, school, or teacher can escape in its limited field the same kind of frustration and punishment encountered by even the greatest teachers, such as Christ, Socrates, and Galileo; the majority laughed or were indifferent as the authorities, convinced of the heresy of new thinking, crucified one, poisoned the second, and disgraced the third. Mental inertia is ever an obstacle to those who teach.

Finally, compensation is needed for exaggerated popular notions of the benefits of education. Its value is immense, but it is neither a cure-all for personal deficiencies nor an automatic assurance of success in life. "Be not over solicitous about education," advised Lord Melbourne, "It may be able to do much, but it does not do so much as is expected from it. It may mould and direct the character,

[2]Albert Schweitzer, *Out of My Life and Thought* (Mentor, 1953), p. 170.

but it rarely alters it."[3] Alas, however, people often expect too much from education, and, despite the success of many with limited schooling but much ability and experience, the school diploma threatens to become a magic union card for life's work. Education badly needs protection from humbug in the form of high-sounding aims and sloppy sentiment which may lead some people to expect too much from the schools, and then, disappointed, to become hostile to the schools and to education itself.

Even with compensations for these characteristics of mass politics, there can still be no magic about state education. The system must always be a secondary factor; the effort of the pupils is the primary factor. Education is a process of *getting* knowledge, not receiving it, and if a pupil will not make the effort to get it no one can give it to him. Those who look to the state to provide an education for their children need remember that the government cannot pass out competence in English, geometry, or carpentry. It can only provide some of the conditions under which the pupils may work.

I have written this book to examine the control of education by the state and the effect of that control on the schools and the teaching profession. It is written in favour of state ownership, on the side of the public schools, and in support of democracy in education. I must dissociate myself from those who criticize the schools in order to undermine the public character of education and in an effort to build up some other form of control of schools. The element we are examining is control; and any control, social, denominational, professional, as well as political, needs careful scrutiny and understanding if the schools are to thrive. I offer criticism and suggest ways of strengthening the public schools because I believe that they should be among the strongest institutions in the nation if they are to serve it to the extent required in this age of overwhelming challenge and uncertain response.

The word "state" has been used throughout the book as meaning the people in political association, including federal, provincial, and

[3]Virginia Cowles, *Edward VII and His Circle* (London: Hamish Hamilton, 1956), p. 23.

municipal governments. A distinction frequently made in educational discussion is to limit the term "state" to a central government and to regard municipalities and their boards and officials as being non-governmental. I use the term in its broadest sense because the influence of politics and governmental administrative practices is generally applicable from the legislature to the local municipal school board.[4]

The thesis of this book is that public enterprise is both necessary and desirable in education, but that, as in other state activities, it should be just public enough to remain enterprise. There is a point beyond which it loses efficiency and freedom. "Government," says the Carnegie Corporation, with the wisdom of long experience, "has its necessary function in support of free schools and colleges and universities; but the success of government, whether federal, state, or municipal, in the field of education, broadly defined, will be in proportion to the degree in which it does *not* dominate."[5]

[4]The pioneering achievements of Egerton Ryerson in establishing a comprehensive state system in Ontario affected every authority from cabinet to school board.

[5]*Statement of the Carnegie Corporation of New York to the Special Committee of Congress to Investigate Tax Exempt Foundations* (July, 1954), p. 2.

2. Politics and the Schools

DOMINATION OF THE PUBLIC SCHOOLS BY THE STATE IS INDICATED BY the direct participation in school affairs of almost every level of government, and this participation is accompanied by the efforts of numerous pressure groups representing all categories of public opinion. The school is thus suspended from the legislature by a long chain of authority with many links: the cabinet, the minister of education, the department of education, the municipal council, the school board, and numerous officials and committees associated with each one. Below a tail chain rattles incessantly, made up of such active bodies as political parties, Home and School associations, and ecclesiastical organizations. The contrast with other public enterprises is striking: in them distribution of authority from top to bottom has a comparatively short span; in education the middlemen are numerous, vocal, and powerful.

State direction of the school system, a prerogative of the provincial governments in Canada, belongs to the legislatures and the municipal councils. The legislature passes the necessary laws and appropriates funds and maintains contact with education through debates on bills, consideration of estimates of expenditure, reports by the minister of education and his officials, and whatever interest individual members may take in the educational affairs of their constituents and friends. In theory the legislature exercises supreme power; in fact it can devote only a limited portion of its time and attention to educational matters and relies on others for advice and action. The municipal council plays a similar role in the local area, passing on much of its responsibility to the school board.

The executive functions in education, the carrying out of laws and the formulation of policy, are in the hands of the cabinet and the school boards. These bodies have full power over the academic policy and most of the business policy of the entire public school system. Like the legislature, however, the cabinet has many other responsibilities, and it can spend only a small part of its time on education. Ministers in departments other than education have their own duties to attend to, and they can scarcely be expected to be familiar with current school matters. Once again, direct responsibility must be passed on to other hands.

In local areas boards of school trustees, consisting of elected or appointed citizens, serve education in a part-time capacity for a limited term. They receive certain powers by statute of the legislature and by-laws of the municipal council. They build and maintain schools, hire teachers and pay part of their salaries, and sometimes, in rural districts, collect school taxes. These powers are today shared with the central government, for its support is essential if necessary money and personnel are to be secured and if general administrative regulations are to be followed.

Four public bodies, therefore—legislature, cabinet, municipal council, school board—share authority over the schools. The work of the provincial and municipal politicians and trustees who comprise them is, in theory, most important, for these men are the representatives of the people who require educational services and pay for them. They are responsible to public opinion, and their policies and actions can be subjected to the open discussions of legislature and local council and to the will of the people at election time. As "laymen" with general experience they are in a position to contribute the direction, suggestions, encouragement, and criticism of persons who see the system as a whole and its effect or lack of effect on the community. All the advantages of control through parliamentary democracy, it would seem, can apply in education.

When we examine the actual operation of cabinets and school boards in educational administration, however, we are struck by two aspects: the uncertain nature of their relationship to the schools and the dubious effects of governmental business practice in education. Their results throw doubt on the practicality of democratic responsibility through direct political control.

The first aspect is created by a paradoxical combination of remoteness and closeness in the connections between the executive and school system. In some respects the executive is separated by a wide gulf from those who perform the functions under its authority. Yet it can intervene readily in the work of the system with immediate and substantial impact. Unfortunately, under present conditions it is impossible to depend upon the executive to be either remote or close at the right time.

All public schools illustrate the remoteness of the educational executive. No one of them has an executive *of its own* with full authority. Unlike a hospital, which has a board identified with the institution itself, or a local church, which has its own elders or trustees or episcopal corporation, the individual school is part of a system, has no power of its own, and receives its policy and direction from a source that controls many other schools. The source has a legal existence but the school and its staff have not. The provincial or municipal government is not interested in any one school, nor is it concerned with education alone; the school board may have several units under its jurisdiction. In such circumstances these bodies are encouraged to look upon the schools and their pupils as statistics and upon the teachers as civil servants whose qualifications and abilities are, at worst, obscure and, at best, classified rather than recognized. To the individual school, on the other hand, "*the* board" cannot be "*our* board" because authority lacks direct and special association with it and interest in it.

This kind of relationship between executive and schools has a far greater effect than is generally recognized. For one thing, it brings an unfortunate element of cold impersonality to the administration of a system of schools and to the function of teaching, and it means that children are sent to, and study in, a place with no identity or authority of its own. Such an impersonal element is certainly not appropriate to education which should be based at all levels on personal recognition, association, and experience. No matter how able politicians or trustees may be, they can do very little to overcome this impersonality as long as there is direct, but remote, governmental control.

Then, too, the relationship makes impossible the application of one of the most sensible principles of administration: that those who determine policy should be well advised by those who carry it out, and that the latter should have the freest possible hand within their terms of reference. The law and regulations for schools do not provide effectively for recognized, direct, and continuous contact between authorities and teachers. There is no legal procedure by which the politicians and trustees can exchange advice and criticism with the staff of a school. The former make their decisions on the basis of their own judgment, the report of some official, or the representations of certain interest groups—and these decisions, usually in the form of "regulations" or "directives," are transmitted to many institutions rather than to one school. The teacher, in turn, receives directions from "higher up"; to him it is "they," not "we," who run the school. This is not to say that authorities should know all about teaching or that teachers should determine policy, but rather that both policy-making and teaching would be more effective if they could be brought into genuine communication at some point in the system.

The gulf between schools and the authorities over them is not sufficiently wide, however, to provide protection against interference in the former from the latter. There is still a unique opportunity for anyone wishing to intervene in negative fashion in the detailed operation of the school system. And it is easy to see why this negative intervention is quite possible: it does not require the assumption of proper responsibility and the close association with those over whom it is exercised that proper direction would involve.

The difficulty is best illustrated by the dangers of political interference with political motivation. Politicians and trustees occupy temporary and part-time positions which they owe to election and appointment, and it is sometimes extremely hard for them to resist powerful pressure upon them. Admittedly they must be responsible to the people they represent, but such responsibility is dangerous if it becomes merely the pleasing of vested interests controlling blocs of votes. Yet only a very strong official will advocate a desirable and necessary policy against the wishes of persons who can defeat him in the next election, and there are minorities with strong views on education who use this advantage to great effect. Interference based on this impulse is present in all forms of public enterprise; in most there are safeguards to prevent or at least to discourage it; in education there are none. Education is particularly vulnerable to purely political pressure, for it is very close to the ambitions, attitudes, prejudices, and rivalries of the people, which vary widely and change continually. As a cultural process, it is more easily frustrated by such pressure than is a technical one, for it can only thrive in an atmosphere of initiative and freedom. "An unceasing struggle must be fought," said the Harvard Committee on General Education in a Free Society, "to free education from a type of direct political control which seeks to impose appointments, restrain the legitimate freedom of teachers, and even dictate what they should teach."[1]

Political interference is not, of course, the only kind of intervention. The large gap between executive and school inevitably encourages others to try to fill the unnatural vacuum in administration. Some of these people, of course, have a genuine and promising interest in the school, and it is unfortunate that they soon find authority so placed that it is difficult for them to actually accomplish anything. But there are many others who wish rather to meddle or to launch crusades or attacks on schools and teachers. As another chapter will indicate more fully, the affairs of the schools are open

[1] *Report of the Harvard Committee on General Education in a Free Society* (1950), p. 25.

for anyone to see and dabble in if he wishes and there is therefore inadequate defence against these approaches. In comparison, hospitals, churches, banks, and other public institutions are closed sanctuaries, in which authority is much more clearly defined and carefully delegated and outside influence can be dealt with in organized fashion. In schools the influence of public opinion is to be expected and is even essential; but here too there must be possible response to its wise judgment and protection against its aberrations.

Too free a scope for all kinds of public opinion in the operation of the school system cannot be justified by the assumption that "education is everybody's business." A moment's thought will show that here is a *cliché* applicable to almost all professions, and that it is not possible to make use of it to intervene irresponsibly in the affairs of other public institutions. Why then should it be used in connection with schools? Sometimes the play of public opinion is justified on the ground that the schools and teachers must serve other institutions and groups but this too is questionable. There is no good reason why education cannot be allowed to serve other activities on its own initiative. No one has yet found a way by which it can serve many masters satisfactorily and be at everybody's beck and call. In trying to do so it is almost forced to dabble in all things and neglect its own imperative responsibilities. Education must function for its own sake as well as for that of others, a point which elected officials, trustees, and pressure groups are all too inclined to forget.

Surely, it may perhaps be said, all public men have a genuine interest in schools and in the pupils. Any such expectation is unduly optimistic, for benevolent attitudes towards education though sometimes obvious are not universal in government. While many politicians have a genuine interest in education and would do all they could to improve it, there are others who are suspicious of it or of anything that smacks of culture. Some of them place political expediency above education; indeed it is often impossible for them to do anything else. Moreover, the possibilities of pressure will often paralyse the executive. Most politicians regard educational problems as potential political dynamite, and will often resort to any tactic to keep them in the background. And experience has taught them that public works, social services, and other "practical" enterprises are better vote-getters than educational improvements. From the purely political standpoint a dormant educational system is much less troublesome than an energetic one and, consequently, activity is often more likely to invite political pressure than inactivity. "Naturally," says the Learned-Sills Report on Education in the Maritime Provinces of Canada, "the effect is to be felt in negative rather than positive forms. Education must 'keep its place'; an aggressive policy . . . is thought to be out of the question for a body that desires reelection; the department of education is managed with whatever proposals a cabinet will consider harmless."[2] Consequently, there is between the executive and the system a no man's land of educational problems which cannot be settled simply because no one desires or dares to deal with them. Effective power cannot be exercised and a series of resulting short-term expedients often brings uncertainty and confusion.

It has to be acknowledged that the frequent lack of exercise of effective power and genuine interest in the schools can be related in part to the peculiar uncertainties of politics. Unquestionably, much can be done for the schools by politicians who have ability, common sense, and an appropriate interest in education. The school system has received many benefits from the administration of such men, and there will always be a number of them in the institutions of government. Yet education does not receive a full share of even their talents, because they simply have not the time to give. They may be further hampered by a precarious tenure of office. It is also unfortunately true that the chances of politics will usually bring into governmental institutions some persons who have mediocre ability, who lack common sense, or who are more concerned with selfish interest than with public welfare. These people can do much harm to the school system either directly through their own mistakes or indirectly through obstruction which frustrates others.

[2]W. S. Learned and K. C. M. Sills, *Education in the Maritime Provinces of Canada* (New York: Carnegie Foundation for the Advancement of Teaching, 1922), pp. 6, 7.

In any system, protection against human weakness is just as important as scope for personal ability. Such protection is not as easily arranged in the system of authority under discussion as one would wish. At the cabinet level it is well known that political availability is just as important as personal ability as a qualification for membership but that political availability is not a guarantee of executive or administrative competence. Consequently, one of the hardest tasks of a premier is to pick a cabinet of able colleagues, especially in small governments where the proportion of cabinet ministers among members of the legislature is high. It takes only one or two indifferent ministers to make things difficult in such an unprotected public activity as education. At the local level, capable school trustees are often extremely difficult to obtain. It is common, even in large cities, for people to take on the responsibility because "they couldn't get anyone else." Many of these do become excellent trustees but, under the circumstances, it is easy for the uninterested, the inept, or the troublesome to find places.

The advantages and disadvantages of political direction are clearly illustrated by the office and powers of the minister of education—the head of the public school system. In practice the legislature and the cabinet determine their policy on the recommendations of the minister and their instructions are given through him. The municipal councils and school boards, in turn, are dependent on him for substantial direction and financial assistance. Outside the government the minister's importance is obvious everywhere, for he has much influence in the cultural processes of his province. Every educational institution, every teacher, every policy is subject to the wide power given him by legislation and orders-in-council. Enterprises in such fields as music, art, and drama are often dependent on his good will for encouragement, facilities, or funds. Much therefore depends on his relations with the cabinet and the legislature which must approve his actions, with the schools which must follow his directions, and with other bodies which might require his co-operation. Like a great thunderbird on a totempole the minister of education overshadows all below. .

When we look more closely into the minister's activities we find a tendency for them to conflict with the main principles of cabinet government. "It is not the business of a Cabinet Minister to work his department," runs Walter Bagehot's famous rule. "His business is to see that it is properly worked. If he does much he is probably doing harm." Policy-making and general direction should be his responsibility; the details should be left to others. Unfortunately, the minister of education all too often finds it difficult to resist going beyond his responsibility and getting into all sorts of activities for which he is unfitted and with which a politician should never be concerned. "We are going to improve our educational system," said the minister of education of one of the larger Canadian provinces, "until the last shreds of this so-called progressive education are gone." This gentleman is a distinguished Canadian and the policy was widely applauded. Nevertheless, the question is surely fair: why should he be called upon to carry out a programme so intimately concerned with a profession and its work?

The reason the minister finds himself in this position is that there is no organization or individual below him in the schools or teaching profession with sufficient responsibility and power. Other ministers head activities in which the government may not have a monopoly, in which the institutions concerned have power of their own, or in which the professions involved are strong. The attorney-general must defer to courts which are independent of him and deal with lawyers in private practice who belong to a strong profession. The minister of health plays only a minor role in the training and licensing of doctors and in the running of hospitals: he would never attempt to issue directives on the treatment of ailments. Ministers of finance or treasurers have a hard-boiled world of business to deal with and they can do little without careful consultation with its leaders. Other ministers are in similar positions; they have power, but there are agencies to check the use of it which are well-informed and influential. But who is there to check a minister of education? The schools and the teachers who are most directly concerned with education have no power whatever and no independence, and the minister can consult, direct, or ignore them at will.

The minister's power as such is not, of course, the only factor in this situation. Much also depends on the personal qualities of the incumbent and on the many uncertain elements of politics. A minister of ability and common sense (and there have been many of them) can give a substantial amount of leadership and thus bring to the school system many advantages of wise executive direction. His talents may be confined, however, by political obstacles such as insufficient prestige, unco-operative colleagues, the pressures of campaigning, and party policy. He may be holding his seat in the legislature by a narrow margin, or be dependent on a pressure group to keep him in office, in which cases he must proceed with caution. What he can do in office depends always on the quality and strength of the government, on his relations with the premier who appointed him, and on the political situation at the moment.

An incompetent minister has, unfortunately, the same power and is in the same political position. He can do irreparable damage because of his own limited abilities and his helplessness against political obstacles. Usually it is the incompetent minister who is least inclined to follow Bagehot's rule and who meddles, without advice or with the wrong advice, in matters of which he knows nothing. He may take himself too seriously if he is not aware, as Lord Acton put it, that "there is no worse heresy than that the office sanctifies the holder of it." He may be holding his office because he was the only politically available person to take it. In theory he "knows what the people want"; in practice he is simply the man who won the majority of votes in a constituency, and his interpretation of public opinion and of needs in education may be at times unreliable. He may have some understanding of educational problems and he may think he is acting for the welfare of the system, but it is easy for him to become impatient with academic matters because, as a politician, he may have an axe to grind, a section of voters or vested interest to please, or a controversy to avoid.

It is possible for a premier to find a minister of education of ability and experience, but in the reality of politics it is not easy because of the minister's position in the cabinet and legislature. His portfolio is generally regarded by politicians as a junior one which is always difficult and often politically embarrassing and which involves control of no patronage and no votes. Experienced politicians tend to avoid it if they can and it is almost invariably assigned to a new and untried member of the cabinet. In 1953, a period when most Canadian provincial governments had been in office for some time, nine out of ten ministers of education were holding their first portfolio. The minister is therefore often an apprentice in the cabinet and his power and influence are necessarily limited until he has gained some experience and seniority. He must argue with senior colleagues for what attention he can secure from the cabinet for educational matters. He has not an easy subject to advocate because the claims of public works, industries, and health and welfare will easily overshadow those of education since the services they provide are more tangible, more popular, and, therefore, politically more interesting and less dangerous. He knows that in terms of votes a mile of paved highway is more productive than a school. He will find that compromise is an important element in cabinet procedure and that it is considered an easy expedient for many educational problems. His ability to obtain benefits and establish policy for his department in the legislature are affected by the same limitations of his office, the same need for winning votes and avoiding controversy, and by the amount of skill he has developed in dealing with the opposition and the back-benchers of his own party. He can never forget that politics, not educational activity, will make his career, a fact which always qualifies his leadership of the school system.

The second striking aspect of the operation of a political executive in the public school system is seen in the application of governmental business practices to education.

An examination of school finance soon indicates the importance of running the school's business affairs properly, so that public funds are spent responsibly and well. It has been widely assumed, therefore, that educational finance should be the exclusive prerogative of the public authorities. This assumption is remarkable in that it is not generally made in other kindred fields. Whereas governmental business practices are appropriate to the tasks which governments are designed to perform *directly*, such as the administration of departments, their suitability for other tasks has long been open to question in this age of expanding state control. It has been accepted, for example, that a government department cannot run directly a hospital, a railway, a power company, or a factory, for it has neither the knowledge nor the facilities to handle the details. The practice today is for governments to entrust such enterprises to semi-independent, publicly owned organizations, and to separate their finances from the treasury, even where public ownership and general responsibility are jealously guarded. This practice, which will be referred to in more detail in a later chapter, has not been adopted in school administration. Ministerial responsibility is rigidly maintained through departmental control; local responsibility is firmly held by municipal school boards and their officials; school finance is mixed with public finance; and no power is left to the schools themselves. School administration is, therefore, purely political, and any concessions to business management are necessarily coincidental.

Proper application of business principles is related to two types of control—one over extravagance and waste which can result from lack of planning and excess ambition, and one over parsimony in essential matters which may not be spectacular. The need for wisdom in school construction, for example, is obvious when the annual investment in it has increased tenfold in two decades. Judgment is necessary in offering courses: it is easy to offer them but it is often difficult to secure money to pay for them and teachers to teach them. Parsimony appears most obviously in the payment of teachers and may also be evident in the provision of equipment. "Making do" can be one of the individual school's chief chores and the departmental accountant and the secretary of the local board of trustees usually see that it attends to it.

The need for sound business sense is especially obvious in planning.

While most other organizations are constantly looking ahead, many school authorities tend to deal only with immediate situations, and the resulting confusion in both personnel management and school finance is unique among community enterprises.[3] A hospital or business which faced in its field anything like the teacher shortage or the prevailing lack of funds would have to draw up a long-term plan, or curtail expansion, or go bankrupt. The planning of a faculty several years in advance, or the purchase of real estate near a school for future expansion are obviously important. But politicians and trustees are temporary officials interested in no one school, and few are able to concern themselves with such long-term projects. Rarely can money be saved for depreciation and future needs; big expenditures are often loaded on the taxpayers all at once and a resulting objection from the public is to be expected. Furthermore, since authorities must include several units and their facilities in one comprehensive budget, they cannot keep weak schools and activities from limiting the strong. Consequently, robbing Peter to pay Paul is one of the most common business practices in public school administration.

A business-like attitude to current educational fashions and pressures is also obviously necessary. Government is always vulnerable to groups and individuals who demand things for which they don't have to pay. School policy should change with the times, of course; but it should not be subjected to every passing public fancy or to the whims of every official. It is peculiarly susceptible to such pressures and it requires protection from the effects of too many of them.

These business problems are the results of mixing school finances with those of other government enterprises. Such problems are inevitable where there is so little regular contact between those who determine policy and raise and spend money, on the one hand, and those who perform the functions for which the policy and the funds are designed, on the other. There is at present no efficient way in

[3]For a public accusation of politics and incompetence in school administration and a demand for the resignation of the authorities concerned, see the *Ottawa Journal*, Nov. 12, 1959.

which the reasonable demands of both sides can be met and the unreasonable demands of both sides frustrated.

The results of an enterprise provide justification for its existence and a measure of its efficiency. We should, therefore, now examine the results of direct political control of the school system and we may do this by a broad general comparison of the state of education with that of other activities, both public and private.

The recent advances made in physical and biological science have been phenomenal. Institutions have grown in size, numbers, and power. The age of the machine is well established. In a number of fields of advance, the state has been involved, as in transportation, electric power, broadcasting, and social services; here governments are performing tasks undreamed of by their predecessors. And the state has been able to keep up with trends in economic, scientific, and social life largely because of its early recognition of the fact that local and professional initiative and independence in these fields were just as important as public responsibility. Such initiative and independence were impossible under political and departmental administration. Consequently, the many new types of government owned, but independently operated, organizations mentioned above were devised to combine the best features of administration and responsibility by means of delegated power to institutions and professions.

The state in the broad field of education is very far behind. In this age man can penetrate outer space but not the hearts of a neighbouring people, control atomic fission but not prevent blowing himself up, circumnavigate the earth in a few hours but not establish a stable international organization. Science has outstripped art; his machines and his organizations have overwhelmed man. One of the main reasons for this unfortunate situation is that education is the weakest of all the activities of the modern state. The plant, the laboratory, the power site are fully developed and efficiently run and their costs are figured in the millions and billions. Beside these schools are poor relations. In local areas the machine has a similar advantage over the mind; from the largest cities to the smallest towns, there is more invested and spent in garages and filling stations for the sale and maintenance of cars than there is in schools for the education of children.

The question is surely one of control. Scientists still do 99 per cent of the work in science; doctors still control medicine; the law is still in the hands of judges and lawyers; engineers are still entrusted with engineering projects; clergymen are still in charge of churches. Teachers, however, are not in charge of education; it is left to the control of politicians, civil servants, and pressure groups, and, consequently, the schools and the teaching profession can exercise little leadership in this age of "universal education." Education thus lags so far behind technology that it seems fair to question whether it is in the right hands.

The refusal to grant power to the schools and the rights of leadership to the teaching profession is defended on the assumption that officials are best able to handle it, which has already been questioned, and also on the principle of democratic responsibility. We have already commented on the desirability of this principle; we must now note the tendency to overemphasize it. Actually of all the weaknesses of the present system of concentrated political power over the schools, the most serious and fundamental, yet in many ways the least obvious, is overemphasis on democratic control because it can so easily lead to totalitarianism. Whatever desirable features are involved, and there are many of them, a democratic society can never ignore with safety the traditional emphasis which the state places on submission to authority. The more comprehensive and detailed is public control of education, the greater is this emphasis bound to be. "The objections which are urged with reason against State education," wrote John Stuart Mill, "do not apply to the enforcement of education by the State, but to the State's taking upon itself to direct that education; which is a totally different thing . . . . A general State education is a mere contrivance for moulding people to be exactly like one another . . . in proportion as it is efficient and successful, it establishes a despotism over the mind."[4] Thus while the people may want the government to control education and even make demands for increases in that control, they should recognize the ultimate end involved. "I believe," said John Ruskin, "that the masses have a right to claim education from their government; but only so far as they acknowledge the duty of yielding obedience to their government."[5] This observation was amply illustrated in our own generation by the use of political monopoly over education in the German schools and universities as an instrument of totalitarian aggrandizement.

This latter type of overt totalitarianism may not seem a threat in a democratic country, but there is, nevertheless, an insidious danger in control getting to the point where the people expect too much from the state and do not do enough for themselves. If dependence on the state goes too far, lack of incentive and initiative in its citizens may result. Then experimentation, competition, criticism, and inventiveness would decline, and the system would lose the spirit and flexibility which are so vital to education. With the pupils the idea would soon prevail that education is to be provided, not worked for, and the coming generation, which is relied on to maintain democratic traditions would not have the proper drive to do so because it would have got into the habit of expecting rather than doing. Ultimately the government would not have what it needs— a free, energetic, thinking body of citizens who will live up to their political principles, not merely profess them, and support their state, not merely obey it.

There is a still greater danger in the extreme "democratic" uniformity of education, which is often demanded as desirable. Admittedly, regulations designed to prevent wide variations in standards and to promote efficient administration are necessary to a certain extent. It is equally necessary, however, to avoid a dead level of mediocrity and an uninteresting pattern of beliefs and methods in which variation and individuality are suspected and crushed. This

[4] J. S. Mill, *Essay on Liberty* (Everyman, 1944), 161.
[5] John Ruskin, *Unto This Last and Other Essays* (Dent, 1938), p. 11.

problem looms large in modern education. "The influence of the State in our daily lives," wrote R. A. Butler when Britain's Chancellor of the Exchequer, "has grown greatly in the past century. Not all these accessions of power are to be deplored. On the contrary, most are to be welcomed . . . . But there is a danger against which we have to guard. The danger is that the State should become all-powerful and the people merely unidentifiable units . . . . We must not allow our children to become like peas in a pod, or units in vast educational factories where their individuality would be lost . . . in the name of sanity and all educational experience, do not let us make the mistake of backing uniformity before everything else."[6]

This view of the state and education invites consideration of the Russian system. In that system the state is dominant; in it, too, educational development has been such as to astonish the world. But comparison between Russian education and ours must be based on a clear understanding of the difference between the political systems. This difference not only makes comparison of the two educational systems unreliable, but also presents a possible explanation of the difference in their results. In Russia everything comes under state control and everyone works for the state; schools and teachers are in the same position as everyone else. In the democracies the parliamentary system acts to limit the state's functions and subordinates the government to the people; their schools and teachers, however, get special state control of a kind to which other services are not subjected. Russia thus runs a totalitarian school system in a totalitarian state; are we not creating a totalitarian school system in a democratic state?

What, then, is the place of politicians and trustees in a democratic school system? Sir Ernest Barker, whose eminence in the field of government is everywhere recognized, answers this question admirably. "It is not the business of law," he wrote, "or of any legal authority, to control the inner life of the process of education. It is only the business of law, and of any legal authority (even if it be called an education authority), to secure the external conditions of a

[6]*The Spectator*, May 20, 1955.

process which, in itself, is necessarily independent of law and legal authority."[7] This principle does not reflect on the character and abilities of politicians and trustees, but states a conclusion about their offices and powers in a system whose purpose is the processing of the mind. If all educational officials in the existing system were replaced with teachers the same limitations would have to apply. Men in authority, no matter who or where they are, display the natural characteristics of human behaviour in the exercise of power. Education is not a special field of political virtue. In approaching it governmental officials should not be obsessed with their own importance; rather, it is suggested, they should concede, as they have already conceded in other fields, that the many inevitable restrictions on their effectiveness may in turn hinder education, and that it and politics do not mix. "It may be a reflection on human nature, that such devices should be necessary to control the abuses of government. But what is government itself, but the greatest of all reflections on human nature? If men were angels, no government would be necessary. If angels were to govern men, neither external nor internal controls on government would be necessary. In framing a government which is to be administered by men over men, the great difficulty lies in this: you must first enable the government to control the governed; and in the next place oblige it to control itself. A dependence on the people is, no doubt, the primary control on the government; but experience has taught mankind the necessity of auxiliary precautions."[8]

The long chain of authority described at the beginning of this chapter was bound, sooner or later, to produce the inexorable operation of Parkinson's law of administration. This dictum concerns people who organize other people's work and in doing so build office hierarchies for purposes of administration rather than for the actual functions involved. In any organization, it states, the number of subordinates multiplies regardless of the amount of work that the staff actually performs. Nowhere is this law more obvious than

[7]Sir Ernest Barker, *Principles of Social and Political Theory* (London: Oxford, 1952), p. 121.
[8]Hamilton-Madison, *The Federalist* (Modern Library ed.), p. 337.

in the school system. Because education is not really suited to political direction and because the state nevertheless does not trust direction to the schools and their teachers, a veritable Pandora's box of officials has been opened and a large administrative class has been released to take control: the "expert" officials, the "educators." Thus bureaucracy, the inevitable accompaniment of too much state control, appears, grows, and thrives. To alter a famous song in *The Gondoliers*:

> Since brass hats now are cheap as sprats
> Inspectors with official chats
> Are plentiful as tabby cats—
> In point of fact too many,
> And deputies crop up like hay,
> Committeemen and such as they
> Grow like asparagus in May,
> Trustees are three a penny.
> On every side directors beam,
> Small beer the superintendents seem,
> With "Home and School" the cities teem
> All round this wide dominion.

3. Back-Seat Drivers

EDUCATIONAL ADMINISTRATORS HAVE BY FAR THE MOST POWER AMONG civil servants in general and within the educational system itself. These officers include deputy ministers, directors of various branches of the departments of education and their assistants, and school inspectors and superintendents. They advise politicians and trustees and transmit executive authority to the schools, control the curriculum and the methods of teaching, direct the normal schools, license the teachers, supervise the construction, maintenance, management, staffing, and inspection of schools, make and enforce classroom regulations, perform office tasks of keeping records, paying staff, and purchasing supplies, and, above all, speak for education to the public. This imposing list of powers reveals an emphasis on administration in education which is without parallel in any other activity in the modern state.

Departments of education are the only departments of government in which the deputy minister is called superintendent, chief superintendent, director, or chief director, and in which his subordinates, even in the clerical grades, follow after with equally impressive titles. They are also the only departments which violate a fundamental rule of government that civil servants should be anonymous, for educational officials enjoy the unusual privilege of speaking in public for both the government and the schools. To the public, no teacher, regardless of ability, can command the prestige of an "inspector" or "superintendent." Even the universities pay tribute to the source of power when they automatically bestow on numerous educational officials the honorary doctor's degrees which are rarely given either to outstanding school teachers, or to officials in other government departments.

With the spotlight on administrators, teachers are in the shadows. Certainly no other profession in the modern state can compare with teaching in respect to the amount of administration. "Administration rather than teaching catches the public eye," writes an eminent authority. "Many administrators have more prestige than they would have as teachers . . . the most important part of the entire education job, the work of the teacher, is too much ignored, too much taken for granted, too little appreciated and too seldom evaluated."[1] It becomes obvious why the idea prevails that the best positions and the greatest opportunities in the educational system lie outside the schools altogether and that teachers wishing promotion should look to administration. Emphasis would seem to be put on the wrong activity, for surely teaching is the primary purpose in the school system and should lead to its own rewards.

We should first ask what effect the great prestige enjoyed by administrators actually has on the school system. In a discussion on this subject it must first be emphasized that administrative talent is not common in any field. Administration is always a difficult art wherever exercised because it requires peculiar combinations of abilities, personal characteristics, and powers. There are, nevertheless, many people who think they know the art, and it is, moreover, a popular activity because it provides an opportunity to direct a function or institution and thus satisfies an urge to command. A major problem in most fields, however, especially those where administration is emphasized, is to find and encourage those who actually have a talent for administration, who respect what they administer rather than merely their own power, and who can be made effectively responsible both for their actions and to their organizations. For administration, like alcohol, can be both bene-

[1]M. E. LaZerte, "Our Problems and Needs," *The B.C. Teacher* (April, 1952).

ficial and intoxicating. The comment is illustrated in a positive way by the excellent work of outstanding administrators, and in a negative way by the doubtful contributions of those whose enthusiasm for administration far exceeds their talents.

This is a proviso of general application, but one cannot fail to be conscious also of certain factors which are characteristic specifically of educational administration. The chief is its peculiar position between the executive authorities and the schools; it has almost exclusive contact with the former and complete dominance over the latter. Politicians and trustees, who can devote only a limited amount of time to education, tend to rely heavily on their administrative officials for advice and for the carrying out of policy. The schools, lacking identity or power of their own, must depend on the same officials for direction. The result is the division of the system into three distinct groups, the executive, the administration, and the teachers, with virtually no regular contact between the first and third and with the second holding the balance of power.

This arrangement is unique in government and in administration generally, and it invites comparison with the usual arrangement of administrative agencies in other fields which is known as "line" and "staff." In hierarchical structures, such as the army and large governmental or business organizations, the policy-making body directly controls the "line" or operation division and the "staff" is purely "an instrument for planning, for study, and for observation, not an instrument of action."[2] The line divisions, in turn, have direct contact with the executive authority and are never directed by staff divisions. In most activities of government the departmental personnel perform the line functions, and the staff functions rest with planning boards, business bureaus, research groups, and the like.

But the school system is different from other public enterprises. Here the line functions are performed not by the department of education or school board staff but by the school principals and teachers. Yet the important contact between the executive and the

[2]L. D. White, *Introduction to the Study of Public Administration* (New York: Macmillan, 1948), p. 31.

line is interrupted by or channelled through staff agencies, with the inevitable results that the executive and teaching divisions do not understand each other and administration is enhanced out of all proportion to its real significance. Consequently, no matter how able administrators may be, they are in a position which prevents them from doing effective work not just because so much is expected of them but because they break that link between those who decide and those who teach which is vital to good administration.

This characteristic of educational administration means that it is external to the body administered rather than internal. With rare exceptions, no public school has its own fully responsible administration, for, like the executive functions, administrative functions are performed for units of many schools. Again there is the sharp contrast with other institutions in the community which are managed largely within themselves. It is, inevitably, difficult for any administrator to visualize his duties properly since he does not belong to the institution, much less work in the profession, under him. He has the power, but he cannot really do the work to full advantage; yet he cannot be held effectively responsible, for he is too easily protected from taking the blame if anything goes wrong. As for the school itself, it lacks that initiative, sense of responsibility, and prestige which can be aided greatly by a strong internal administration.

It should not be surprising, therefore, if officials are inclined to look upon educational administration from the standpoint of administration rather than from the standpoint of teaching. Nor is it surprising that those training for the profession in normal schools are being prepared for subordinate roles and are treated, in the words of one professor of "education," "merely as prospective teachers whose role in administration and supervision will be that of the administered and the supervised."[3] Officials tend to regard administration from the standpoint of the management of a system rather than the running of individual schools with individual problems or assets.

[3]A. Tremblay, "Brief to Conference of Deans and Professors of Educational Administration and Supervision," Toronto, June 15, 1955.

Why not have common standards, curricula, salaries, and examinations under government control through departments of education and school boards and under the direction of superintendents and inspectors? Some other answers will be developed in subsequent pages, but it can be pointed out for the moment that a large number of other institutions in society, such as churches, business firms, hospitals, banks, and professional groups, seem to be managed effectively through their own internal administration and either find mutually acceptable common standards or pursue differing policies which they and the public readily accept. Is it possible that education today is too much system and not enough school?

The possession of all this power by educational administrators is one of the most interesting yet alarming phenomena in modern government, violating as it does the basic principle that such personnel should be "on tap, not on top." Even if all of them had the highest qualifications, the arrangement would be dangerous, for no one man, group, or school of thought can exercise such power without eventually resorting to dogma, domination, and intolerance of criticism. The dogma is obvious from even a casual reading of pedagogical research and publication; unlike other fields of knowledge, pedagogy permits slight variation in fundamental opinion and little opportunity for other disciplines to make contributions to it.

How far the domination has gone is revealed by an official of the Canadian Education Association. After a survey of the ideas of superintendents of schools themselves, this official stated that the superintendent "perceives himself, as, on the one hand, advising the central authority on local needs and supervising and administering the educational policies of the Board of Trustees, and, on the other, advising the Board of Trustees and supervising the educational policies of the central authority. In his actual role, the superintendent perceives himself as a line and staff officer for both the Department of Education and the Board of Trustees."[4] Surely a more confused interpretation of principles of administration can scarcely be found.

[4] C. P. Collins, "The Provincially Appointed Superintendent of Schools," *The B.C. Teacher* (Nov., 1959), p. 93.

The depressing effect of this kind of administration on teachers and schools, seems inevitable, as is indicated by a retiring principal of a large city school:

The present policy of appointing supervisory supernumeraries, directors, supervisors, special counsellors, and counsellors suggests teachers are comparatively unimportant, though needed to relieve mother of her duties of supervising luncheon children who should be eating at home, to collect milk and soup money, take attendance, and make the routine morning's report of all absentees to the principal's office, make out involved report cards, teach the material in one or two subjects, and do much paper work in connection with standardized tests often designed and set by people who never taught school.[5]

The domination is illustrated still further at the highest official level in the annual report of a provincial Superintendent of Education.

The general lines of our public teaching are strictly fixed by the course of studies ... which comes from the higher authorities ... a body of directives which it is the duty of each inspector to respect and apply. Each environment may have its own conception of the details relating to any one system, but the welfare of some hundreds of thousands of children cannot permit of any whimsical interpretation according to the various viewpoints of this one and that. The very first goal of our official course of studies is to found our school system on fundamental and immutable principles which it would profit no one to change. ... Our course of studies, thus conceived in its essence as in its functions, is the *vade mecum* of the inspectors, because every day they must see to its application and to the observance of both its spirit and letter.[6]

The dangers of such an outlook, which appears general in many provinces, are indicated by the questions which the quotation immediately provokes: Who are the "higher authorities"? When is a viewpoint a "whimsical interpretation," and who decides? What are the "fundamental and immutable principles which it would profit no one to change," and who is able to interpret them? Unfortunately for this theory, higher authorities are often wrong; many great ideas, discoveries, and institutions were originally considered to be whimsical interpretations; and an established principle

[5]S. Meadows (former principal of Simon Fraser School, Vancouver), in *The B.C. Teacher* (Nov., 1959), p. 95.
[6]*Report of the Superintendent of Education, Province of Quebec* (1952–3), p. 36.

can be wrong just as easily as right. The result of this authoritarian administration can be seen behind a plea in an editorial of a magazine for teachers in the same province as the last official quoted above: "The quality chiefly needed, now as always, in educational administration is common sense. Yet how all but inaudible at times is its voice amid the futilities and frustrations of administrative routine."[7]

The intolerance of discussion and criticism on the part of educational administrators in both Canada and the United States has assumed the proportions of a national scandal. It is almost without parallel in the entire structure of government. Most politicians and civil servants expect discussion and criticism as a matter of course and parliamentary government is especially designed to permit argument. Most university disciplines permit discussion and acceptance or rejection of new theories, methods, and ideas among those who teach. In education, however, there is no real opportunity for constructive criticism to be brought to bear on the administration. Effective power is heavily concentrated in its hands, advisory committees are of little value: one inspector's opinion can there overcome the ideas of fifty teachers simply because the department will have the final decision. Indeed, the individual teacher can say little or nothing, for he is not in a position to be frank when his job, prospects of promotion, and salary depend so much on the goodwill of officials. Furthermore, even if suggestions are made to the administration, there is no guarantee that they will ever reach politicians or trustees for there are many ways in which they can be suppressed. A parallel situation is obvious within the universities, where it is difficult for scholars outside the departments of "education" to make their contributions to the subject of teaching in the secondary and primary schools. In most fields a responsible critic can be heard respectfully whether he is ultimately right or wrong. Yet Dr. Hilda Neatby and Professor A. E. Bestor, for example, who were heard respectfully by the public and by the teachers, whether they agreed with the authors or not, found their ideas, characters, and abilities subjected by professional "educators" to an official scorching which

[7]*The Educational Record*, Quebec, vol. LXXI., no. 4 (Autumn, 1955), p. 196.

was not only unworthy of education but also illustrative of many of the things the two authors condemned.

The opinions and policies of administrators can be valuable; so can those of teachers, politicians, and trustees if there is sufficient scope for them to develop. Education lives by the free expression of the ideas of all who are interested in it. But when administrators are dominant and vocal and all doctrine and policies must percolate through them, only their interpretations will have a chance of adoption. "What is really wrong with our Canadian school system," says an eminent scholar, "is . . . its domination by [an] interlocking directorate of orthodox bureaucrats in the provincial departments of education and exponents of orthodox doctrine in the colleges of education. It doesn't much matter what that orthodox doctrine is at any given moment. What is wrong with it is that it is laid down from above as the authoritarian party line. What most needs to be attacked is not the philosophy of these men but their power."[8]

Such an excess of administration often assists a tendency to emphasize its mechanics. Red tape is a traditional weakness in any large organization and officials can easily convince themselves of the necessity of forms, reports, statistics, inspections, and instructions, and appear busy and important with routine. Divisions like to accumulate power and thus build little hierarchies. Functions appear and grow just for the support of the organization, and passing letters and files back and forth, "seeing" one another, attending committee meetings, and protecting their own power for the sake of themselves often become the chief occupation of those who run the official treadmill. All the standard studies of the civil service and of business management describe this tendency and suggest ways of confining it so that the extent of administration will be in logical proportion to the size and functions of the organization as a whole.

One can expect such a danger with educational administrators too. Some take office routine just seriously enough to be of some help to the schools. But many others go beyond the happy balance

[8]Frank H. Underhill, *Transactions of the Royal Society of Canada*, vol. XLVIII, Series III (June, 1954).

and fail to realize how, in education more than in most activities, excess bustle in "the office" can quickly obstruct the work and try the patience of the staff. In many cities and towns the superintendent of schools appears to do everything possible to foster the impression that the schools cannot get on without him. Parents soon learn who the boss is; they are often encouraged to by-pass the staffs of the schools and bring their problems to the official level. Report cards often contain messages, not from the principal or teacher, but from the superintendent of schools; and even Christmas greetings have been sent to parents from the superintendent on behalf of principals and teachers. Under such arrangements the office soon assumes the importance which should belong to the classroom. The result is inevitable: "A variety of influences," writes one authority, "has produced a situation to which headmasters react, according to their temperament with exasperation, bitterness, or despair, and which, at the very least, calls for serious and thorough investigation. . . . I do not suggest that my friends in the Ministry of Education and in the office of the local education authorities spend their days and nights deliberately designing ways of limiting the liberty of those who live and work in the schools. But as a matter of practical fact that is what happens, very largely by accident and very slightly by design."[9] No matter how able an administrator may be, he cannot overcome the fact that, because he is not a real part of a school, his power can make his mere presence detrimental to the initiative and effective influence of the school.

It might well be expected that stress on office functions would encourage the tendency of routine to block new ideas and practices. Education always needs imagination and innovation, which must come from the schools if they are to be effective at all. But change is often unpopular with officials unless it is initiated by them, and good ideas and practices are frequently opposed because they are not compatible with existing routine, or perhaps because they cannot be applied to all schools on a large scale. Thus the idea is too

[9]J. F. Wolfenden, "Intellectual Freedom and the Schools," in Dobinson (ed.), *Education in a Changing World* (Oxford, 1951), p. 51.

easily fostered that things are done right only if officials do them. This is of course a familiar weakness in civil service affairs. "The sphere in which the civil service is free to act imaginatively," writes Dr. Corry, "and explore the way to new pinnacles of achievement is very narrow. . . . The civil servant at the lower levels of authority who deals with living persons and concrete situations is immersed in rules, precedents, and instructions. It requires great circumspection to obey them all and his caution may make him almost immobile. . . . The civil servant who will not stay in the rut of routine lives dangerously. In the rut, there is safety and peace."[10] The ruts are very deep in education, and there is a resulting tendency to keep everything quiet at all costs, to crush dissent or complaint, and to favour the conformer and silence the reformer. Consequently, the theme of the average official report or speech is "all's well," and the suggestions and criticisms, which nevertheless are numerous today, are coming from outside the school system.

There can be no defence for such practices in the theory of democratic responsibility. When the administration gets such an emphasis the opinions or policies of "the government" which is supposed to be responsible to the people will mean nothing more than the views of minor officials trying to interpret regulations. The element of "responsibility" then becomes purely theoretical. In practice, many people who have to deal with the schools cannot use the ordinary methods of man-to-man relations, but find themselves dealing with a machine with all the usual tendencies to red tape and buck-passing. As a result, the school system is one of the most difficult of all public enterprises to do business with and many necessary improvements are therefore delayed or neglected.

"Professions," said George Bernard Shaw, "are conspiracies against the laity," an opinion sometimes used against a tendency to exaggerated specialization within them. This tendency is often illustrated in administration by an attitude of exclusiveness, a potentate complex, the use of jargon, and, ultimately, the taking of

[10]J. A. Corry, *Democratic Government and Politics* (Toronto: University of Toronto Press, 1946), pp. 300, 303.

power too seriously. Many officials in education have never succumbed to it, but enough of them have to arouse attention and resistance to it.

The tendency can be illustrated in the fact that educational administrators have actually developed a profession of their own and are particularly exclusive about it. Thus the educational system has two professional groups, the administrators who, in Canada, call themselves the Canadian Education Association, and the teachers, who belong to the Canadian Teachers' Federation. Each group has its own journals which reflect the opinions and interests of their readers, and its own conventions at which there is very little opportunity for association and discussion outside a limited circle. Surely this is a separation which must be deplored. This professional exclusiveness has gone so far that administrators rarely belong to associations of historians, chemists, or others interested in the subjects which are taught; and, extraordinary as it may seem, there are very few of them in the membership of organizations whose primary interests are the institutions and problems of government. Exclusiveness has indeed reached the point where officials assume the word "education" to describe their courses, degrees, and profession. They call one another "educators"; the rank and file are simply teachers. No other administrators associated with professions are in such a position; hospital administration, for example, is not yet called "medicine"; and national bar and engineering organizations are not yet controlled by departments of justice or public works. In education alone does administration become synonymous with the function of the entire system.

There is no great difficulty in finding illustrations of this point. At the individual level, it is common to hear an "educator" argue with friends in other disciplines as though he alone was qualified to give expert judgment on pedagogy, or perhaps smile indulgently at the naïvity of the comments thereon of his "academic" colleagues. At the group level there are many illustrations. One might be the description "leading educators from all the Provinces of Canada" given by the Canadian Education Association to a conference

designed to give "inspiration in educational leadership"; it consisted
almost entirely of administrators of education.[11] Another is the
establishment of the "Canadian Education Association—Kellogg
Project in Educational Leadership" which is "designed to assist
school superintendents and inspectors in their task of providing
educational leadership in Canadian communities." The project is
unquestionably a worthy one, but why should it be confined to
administrators? Would it not be much more useful and informed if
it comprised responsible leaders among school principals, teachers,
and trustees? Can administrators by themselves form useful policies
for, or make reliable judgments on, the management of a system in
which they perform a purely tertiary function? Are superintendents
and inspectors really the people who should be "providing educational leadership in Canadian communities"? In other fields it is the
executive and practising personnel, and rarely the administrators,
who give the leadership. "L'école c'est moi" might be suggested as a
fitting motto for administrators of education today.

It goes without saying that the most important aspect of the
functioning of educational administration is its effect on the school
and its teachers, and we might now look at the question from this
standpoint. Here once more actual practice is quite different from
current theory and popular conception. We have seen that it is
generally accepted that the government and the school board must
have some control over the school and that the department of
education and local superintendents and inspectors should provide it.
At the same time, it has been suggested that it is questionable
whether officials *outside* the schools are better able to serve as the
necessary link between the authorities and the schools than those
who are *inside* the schools. The significance for the schools themselves
is obvious. Administrators today cannot speak *for* the schools; they
must speak *about* them or *to* them. Consequently, the schools do not
have spokesmen who can adequately express their needs, and the

[11]*The Superintendency—Leadership in Action*, C.E.A. Booklet (1955), p. 6. The language and
assumptions of this booklet might well be studied in this context.

executive gets only second-hand and one-sided advice and requests which are easy to misinterpret, ignore, or forget.

The fact that administrators speak *to* the schools rather than for them has an inevitable effect on their relations with school personnel. The functions of a superintendent or inspector of schools are popularly conceived as including the interpreting and enforcing of regulations, and the giving of advice and assistance to principals and teachers. Trustees look to him as their executive officer; the department of education usually regards him as the expert in the field, the local interpreter of education to schools and the public: he is an official with duties. The school personnel, on the other hand, cannot help but regard him as an outside individual with power, whose personal qualities rather than official status and real knowledge and judgment rather than formal administrative titles are all-important to them. This distinction is essential in assessing the real usefulness of the administrator's work. For what he does in actual practice is often quite different from what he is supposed to do because administration, in the dominant position it holds in education, requires an exceptionally experienced and sensible person. Under such circumstances, the accepted theory of educational administration breaks down if an unusually gifted person is not available; if he is available the chances are his leadership would be far more effective *inside* the school. Nor is the ability or lack of ability of the administrator the only factor. There is among most professional people a general dislike of "being watched," and teaching is no exception. Weak teachers may be comforted by it, but able teachers understandably find it difficult to endure over-zealous supervision. Even trying to be helpful is difficult for outside administrators and few people can carry it off well. Yet the supervisory activities of departments of education and superintendents' offices seem to increase steadily. "I see a growing tendency," writes one educationist, "for departments of education to tell teachers what is to be taught. Not directly, but indirectly, and the indirect method is the more powerful."[12]

There are those who would claim that administration is needed as

[12]M. E. LaZerte, in *Alberta Teachers Association Magazine* (May, 1955), p. 9.

a compensation for poor teachers. Surely this idea is illogical and indeed dangerous because it amounts almost to a condoning of weaknesses and because it removes the element of responsibility from teaching. Society gives to its doctors, lawyers, engineers, clergymen, and other servants a different sort of trust. Far greater care is taken in the selection of candidates, much power is given to the professions themselves, and they are left to their work with a minimum of public direction and supervision. Even the politician, the most public of all public servants, is unlimited in his actions compared to the teacher. One suspects therefore, that the need for so much administration would be greatly decreased if more emphasis were placed on recruiting good teachers than on keeping an eye on mediocre ones.

Some officials may be heard to say that they are fully aware of the limitations of administration and would like to do everything possible to encourage school personnel to assume their own responsibilities so that they themselves may act more like advisers or consultants than inspectors. They go on to complain that in many instances local initiative cannot be roused. But surely the difficulty here is that the school authorities can exercise no real power and therefore have no incentive. The emphasis on power at the top could be expected to result in lack of energy in the schools. Moreover, as later pages will discuss, the present centralized control can often encourage weak schools and teachers to be weaker still.

Having said all the foregoing about the dangers of administration today, one might still hope that a gifted group of people might in actual practice circumvent them. This prompts a consideration of the education, experience, and personal characteristics presently required of those who occupy the positions and exercise the powers. For the theory of administration can be carried out in practice only if the quality, training, and experience of the personnel match the responsibilities involved.

Preparation for careers in public administration has been the subject of much study in universities and in the government service, and many useful principles have evolved. Administrators have appeared with all kinds of backgrounds: in the humanities, in the sciences, in the social sciences, and in professional studies. Their success has been variously interpreted as coming from broad cultural experience, technical training, or just innate administrative ability and common sense. Certainly there is no one formula by which an aspirant can become an accomplished administrator, for the responsibilities and conditions he may encounter are infinite in their variety and effect; yet there are a few guides.

> I accept the obvious fact [wrote one leading authority on the training of public servants] that in the modern state those who exercise administrative authority increasingly come to wield a crucial power which affects my liberties and your liberties, my amenities of life and your amenities, and by their decisions are helping to shape profoundly the environment wherein we live. . . . They cannot escape from giving advice to their political chiefs. As a consequence of their strategic position for exerting wise influence, they should receive as much liberal education as possible to help them in developing intellectual curiosity, flexible minds, and, most important of all, broad sympathies backed by imagination.[13]

This description of responsibility and qualifications for it is obviously applicable to educational administration, whether at the deputy minister's level or in the superintendent's office.

A remarkable phenomenon in the public school system, however, is the fact that a liberal education receives less stress than a degree in "education," regardless of its quality, and the latter is so essential for admission to administration that by means of it this part of the school system becomes virtually a closed shop. The executive of most organizations is advised by officials with varying backgrounds, and develops a policy upon which differing viewpoints have been brought to bear. A large bank, insurance company, railway, or government department, for example, has in its administrative hierarchy a combination of talents recruited from various activities and backgrounds. Would not this practice seem applicable to education where the field of reference is so wide? But the tendency is to recruit the higher officials from one source—the pedagogy—

[13]Alexander Brady, "The Training and Development of Administrators," in *Proceedings of the Institute of Public Administration of Canada* (1952), p. 320.

trained specialists from schools of "education." Despite the fact that "education" is only one limited discipline in education proper, and regardless of what administrative talent there might be without the label, it is the one qualification without which admission to official circles is virtually impossible. This astonishing situation is unique among all the business, professional, and governmental activities in the modern state.

A B.Ed. or M.Ed. or D.Ed. with emphasis on methods or administration sounds impressive of course, but is there actually any more magic in it than there is in a degree in hotel management or hospital administration? Degrees in administration in any field are useful only in so far as they enable their holders to deduce administrative principles and practices from a wide variety of knowledge and experience associated with the field in which they will work. The effort of taking them is worth-while only if they provide an opportunity for securing knowledge which cannot readily be obtained from equivalent effort on the job or in private study. For it is not merely a knowledge of a few principles of administration which makes an administrator, but his general knowledge, his experience, his character and personality, and, above all, his devotion, not to administration, but to his profession. All disciplines and experiences have provided backgrounds for eminent administrators in all walks of life. Degrees in "education" are thus only one of many means by which administrators can be trained. The study of educational administration can be useful, but there would seem to be no basis for the common assumption that one is qualified for it when one "takes a course" in it or that one cannot be proficient without taking the course. "The university graduate in the civil service," writes a distinguished public servant and educationist, "should be able not only to master the practical problems of administration, but to see them against a wide background of knowledge of history, institutions, and philosophy."[14] This background is essential if the administrator is to perform his duties with judgment, imagination, and

[14]W. A. MacIntosh, "Should We Have Specialized Degrees in Public Administration Given by Universities?" *Proceedings of the Annual Conference of the Institute of Public Administration of Canada* (1949), p. 29.

humanity. Without it he is liable to become a mere follower of routine bogged down in mechanics and regulations.

A particular example might be pointed to here. The lack of knowledge of public affairs, for instance, is often an obvious weakness in those aspiring to degrees in "education." If they are to be trained in educational administration as such, it would seem that officials should know something about government and public affairs in order to advise their superiors properly and relate education to other matters. Such a background can be secured by either study or experience or both. Yet many educational officials have little or no knowledge of this most important aspect of their work. Political science, economics, public administration, commerce, and allied subjects, which are recognized as important in other departments of government, have no space in the graduate or undergraduate preparation of "educators." They have not secured a sufficiently broad background of general studies and experience with which they may build a knowledge of government while in office or which might encourage them to participate in governmental affairs outside their own department. This last point is illustrated within the civil service by the fact that in many places educational officials tend to take virtually no part in the general functions of government.

It is difficult, unfortunately, to ensure both a liberal educational background and a detailed study of "education" within the same college programme. There are normally only twenty courses required for a student's first bachelor's degree and three to five for a second bachelor's degree or a master's degree, and every course in "school management," "curriculum development," "guidance," and the like displaces one in the subjects which give a liberal education. A candidate who takes such specialized courses consequently tends to scatter his other studies, to do a little bit of everything and not much of anything, and may end up with only a superficial background for his managing, developing, and guiding. And even in "education" courses time and opportunity for adequate study are limited. Educational psychology and school administration furnish two of many examples. Psychology itself is a complex and demanding subject requiring adequate background and much study and it can be extremely dangerous if its students take a smattering of it too seriously. Yet many "education" students take a hodge-podge of "educational psychology" with little or no previous study of psychology itself. At best this is only an elementary introduction to a vast field; at worst it is a means by which some officials can assume the role of "specialists" and eventually force naïve theories and practices, or perhaps *the* theory and *the* practice, on the school system. A course in "school administration" is all too often an elementary coverage of a few simple practices which is scarcely worthy of academic or professional credit rather than a thorough study of institutions and administration generally. Graduate study and research in "education" are open to the same objection. Pedagogy theses and articles in general do not come up to the standards recognized in graduate faculties and professional groups and are often mysterious, meaningless, or misleading to both teachers and laymen. These points contribute to the situation described by one professor of "education": "Whatever the reason," he wrote, "it is unfortunate that professional leaders should not have earned a greater measure of respect and this is a problem with which one might hope their associations would be more concerned in future."[15]

"Educators" will often point out in answer to criticism that an administrator does not have to be competent in the subject-matter of what he administers. A good hospital administrator, they would say need not know medicine. Inquiry would tell them that the hospital administrator has no control whatever over the theory and practice of medicine; the educational administrator, however, is not held within the generally accepted limits of administration and therefore needs much more than a limited background in technicalities.

What now of the experience administrators can acquire? It might be expected that an administrator would have obtained a working knowledge of the schools and of teaching after (or before) his other

[15]David Munroe, "Professional Organizations in Canadian Education," in Katz (ed.). *Canadian Education Today* (McGraw-Hill, 1956), p. 228.

training. Some of them have because they have had successful careers as teachers and keep in close touch with what goes on in the schools. Although all successful teachers don't inevitably make good administrators, the value of teaching experience and knowledge is obvious wherever it exists. But experience can be less effective than might seem possible, for reasons which deserve far more attention than they get.

The first is that administrators, once they cease to teach, tend to lose all direct contact with the actual process of dealing with boys and girls. They are remote from the main activity of their system. Once a teacher gives up teaching he soon loses the "feel" of the classroom and the knowledge of the day-to-day behaviour of children and it becomes very easy to look upon teaching as a method or procedure and upon children as statistics. Everyone knows how impractical childless people, and often grandparents, can be about the problems of bringing up children when they have no direct responsibility; this can apply also to the educational official who forsakes the classroom for the office. Just as significant is his declining acquaintance with the demands of the subjects being taught; one of the major occupational hazards of administration is a temptation to neglect one's own professional competence and the developments in one's own subject in the busy round of administrative detail. This substitution of administration for professional work and knowledge on the part of educational officials is quite unusual, even in the civil service. The more usual procedure elsewhere is to alternate a spell of duty at a desk with one in the field, to combine administration with practice, or, when responsible for administration only, to work under the direction of, or in intimate association with, the professional group concerned.

The second of the two limitations in the value of experience gained by administrators is actually common to all administration, but, unpleasant as the thought may be, it seems to be especially applicable to education. People who are failures in their work and who seek to justify themselves, and others who, without obvious natural qualifications, have an urge to run something often go into administration. Perhaps a flair for administration will reveal itself and offset other weaknesses, but, more often in such cases, the ability to administer is not as strong as the desire. In the school system it is too easy for such people to work themselves up purely by seniority, by special personal relations, or by "taking a course": after all it is not the profession itself that appoints them, but politicians and trustees who can hardly be expected to choose wisely at all times. Officials of this type have not only made many mistakes, but they have also provided discouraging examples to teachers who are supposed to follow their direction and to able young people who consider teaching as a career.

It would seem to labour the obvious to say finally that the character of the person involved must be considered along with training and experience in any estimate. No technical training will guarantee those intangible qualities of personality such as honour, judgment, vision, and especially patience. No courses or degrees in "education" will provide them. "A place sheweth the man," wrote Bacon, "and it sheweth some to the better and some to the worse." Consequently, the emphasis on specializing in "education" and on the mere possession of technical qualifications as necessary preliminaries to official appointment seems unreliable.

All these limitations in the training of educational officials are not sufficiently well known to the public to whom a bachelor, master, or doctor of "education" implies something special regardless of the standards involved. It must be emphasized again that there are unquestionably some able administrators; but does not the fact that all tracks lead relatively unimpeded into administration and none lead out indicate that there should be more safeguards against the doubtful ones either in their training or in their subsequent work? Is it not strange that administration is entrusted to an exclusive group when a similar practice is not followed in other government departments or in the professions? Perhaps an important reason is, again, the separation of the authorities at the top from the schools who are administered.

The whole problem of educational administration revolves, therefore, around its great power and its primary location in the school system. The main driving power within the system itself should surely be teaching, with policy-making secondary in importance and administration tertiary. When these forces are not marshalled according to their importance or when they are allowed to interfere with one another, the system will not work properly. There are many signs that administration is not in its proper place. The educational official might well seem to be like a back-seat driver. He rides in comparative opulence, comfort and dignity, he does the talking and gives the orders, but, nevertheless, he does not do the work or bear the responsibility on which the success of the school system ultimately depends.

4. Convoy at Half Speed

THE OBJECT OF ALL THE ATTENTION FROM POLITICIANS AND ADMINISTRA-
tors already described is the public school. Certainly no other institution has so many august sponsors so closely associated with it. We
should now examine the school itself in order to see the actual
operation of this direct state control.

The public school is, to use a phrase introduced earlier, the
community's chief agency for telling people what to do. Institutions
and individuals everywhere, as has been said, like to perform this
function, but with most of them it is an activity which they can take
up when in an expansive mood and drop when they are confronted
with the inevitable oppositions of human nature. The school, however, is set up especially for the task, and its teachers are expected to
give a continuous flow of information and advice to everybody's
young hopefuls. One would suppose, therefore, that the school
would be one of the most respected public institutions, that it
would manage its affairs responsibly and well, that its teachers would
be able citizens thoroughly familiar with the subjects they talk about,
and that their salaries and working conditions would be so satisfactory that appointments to the staff would be eagerly sought.
Any such supposition would, however, be pure fancy. The individual
school has no power of its own; salaries and working conditions are
generally far below the standards expected in other institutions; the
turnover in staff is high and replacements are difficult to find; many

teachers lack adequate qualifications to teach. Some schools, of course, are able to do their work tolerably well where local conditions are at all favourable, but the conditions in most of them are in striking contrast to what the public expects them to do.

Perhaps the reason may not be hard to find. With so much control from others, everybody runs the school but its staff. With no identity, executive, and administration of its own, it actually has less legal status, and fewer functions and powers than a local general store. Public officials control all academic matters, from the training of teachers to the determination of the number of pages of arithmetic to be covered in each grade, and all business matters, from the construction of the building to the purchase of a five-cent eraser for the kindergarten teacher. This situation is often dignified with the title "democratic education," yet there is no more obvious denial of prevailing democratic ideas of self-government in politics and free enterprise in business and professional life.

The main duty of the schools in this position of subserviency must obviously be to obey instructions. Each school receives regulations and orders from outside, follows the directions of a departmental curriculum, and adheres to the sets of facts and opinions given in official textbooks. The staff do not have councils with legal status and jurisdiction over teaching matters; instead "workshops" have been devised to allow discussion which the department overhears. The principal of a school often has little more than a nodding acquaintance with the trustees who decide his school's policy. Should he wish to offer them advice it must be carefully screened through a superintendent; should anything go wrong in his school, however, the screen dodges and he must take the full blame. His authority might be compared to that of a floor walker and clerk. Teachers are always subject to scrutiny: inspectors, superintendents, and even, in some places, such extraordinary visitors as "class mothers" drop in from time to time to observe them at work and report what they see. Indeed, impressing visitors is one of the important chores and greatest time-wasters in most schools. Imagine a government inspector looking over a doctor's shoulders at an operation or a "parish mother" dropping in at the rectory to talk over next Sunday's sermon with the clergyman! Yet it is so easy to interfere with the schools; almost anyone with an axe to grind and an acquaintance on the board can create suspicion and cause turmoil. Practices can be forced on the schools from above: but when the staffs seek improvements they encounter a kind of educational law of gravity which dictates that forces must act downward rather than upward. It is surely no exaggeration to state that in too many instances only a pedagogical Houdini could free himself from the many bonds that limit the freedom to teach.

The business administration of schools appears on examination just as illogical, and indeed a large proportion of the rising cost of education might well be traced to this cause. There is no real budget for each individual school; the financial dealings for each are instead submerged in general funds for a group. Thus if one school requires the use of extensive funds, others in the same community must do without; or, what is worse, if there is not enough money to provide all schools with a certain service or equipment, none will get it. Contracts are awarded by a common board of trustees or a department rather than by an individual board of a school, and this can often be wasteful because people tend to work very differently for a disembodied public authority than they do for an individual or distinct group. The indirect management encourages unjustifiable parsimony or wasteful extravagance: schools are perpetually short of money for services, equipment, repairs, and salaries; at the same time when the authorities in a school get money unexpectedly they are often so unaccustomed to dealing with it that the shock and surprise send them into a spree of foolish spending. No one school can save, invest, or plan for itself; a long-term financial policy for it is impossible. Its day-to-day business is inevitably obstructed by delay and red tape: the purchase of a new five-dollar school bulletin board, for example, often requires all the solemn negotiations of a million-dollar transaction. There is no petty cash in most schools for even the most trifling expenditures.

Is it not to be expected that the operation of this system would affect the status of the school? Constantly begging or doing without, and with inadequate control over their own affairs, they can easily be treated with condescension by their community. They are largely excluded from the public-spirited donations of business firms and wealthy citizens because no one wants to give money to the government and because no one can really be sure, except by contributing specifically to the prize list, that a gift will be spent wisely or that it will not mean the government's cutting down on its own obligations because of the gift. Collections are frequently taken up in schools, and some Home and School groups act as ladies' aid societies, purchasing books, audiovisual equipment, furniture, and the like: why should these not be provided by the school authorities? Such assistance does not give the impression of co-operation and service as it does in private institutions like universities and hospitals; in public schools it is a kind of charity which emphasizes, not institutional spirit, but prevailing poverty and official carelessness. As a result of their financial position, schools have something of the outlook of teen-aged boys without pocket money—naïve in business and over-dependent on and impatient with their superiors.

This system of perpetual subjection must surely be the most inefficient that could be devised because the amount of direction and rigidity harms the intellectual freedom and professional pride so necessary to real teaching and restricts the exercise of responsibility and judgment which is needed for sound business administration. Frank and confidential inquiry among teachers and casual reading of teachers' magazines both have indicated the problem. Even so unexpected a source as a Columbia Teachers' College professor of "education" describes the dangerous results of the prevailing form of administration:

The centralized system assumes control virtually over all aspects of education —the enactment of laws, decrees, and regulations, the limits of compulsory attendance, the establishment and closing of schools, the character of the school buildings, the preparation and certification of teachers, the curricula and courses of study and even methods of instruction in all types of schools, standards of achievement, textbooks, the prescription of salary scales, local administration, and the internal management of schools. Bureaucracy omits no detail, so that when the teacher confronts the pupils in a classroom, sometimes decorated and adorned according to regulations, he becomes practically the mouthpiece of the central authority, a skilled craftsman very frequently but hewing to the line. Now the question which at once arises is whether this is education or propaganda; whether such a system does not destroy the character of the school as a human institution and of instruction as the impact of mind upon mind. Because the essence of such a system of administration is mechanization, the results are often mechanical, rigid, and formal, and superficially the pupils acquire a certain body of content which is neither their own nor their teachers'; it is in such systems that mass education is run at its worst. What is mechanized tends to be destroyed; what is over-organized tends to be killed.[1]

It is strange that the public should expect education to be administered properly under conditions which would not be so generally tolerated in other professional activities. Why, for example, have objections so consistently raised against state religion and state medicine not been used on behalf of the schools? Fanciful though the illustration might seem, we can imagine what would happen if a community ran its churches as it does its schools. There would be a "church board" in the municipal service and a "superintendent of churches" managing all of them from a central office. A governmental "department of religion" would lay down regulations for training clergy, prescribe hymns, prayers, and texts, issue a "sermons curriculum," and suggest programmes for Sunday schools, wolf cubs, and ladies' aids. There would be directors of missionary activities and church suppers in the department, as well as experts specially trained in the techniques of baptisms, weddings, and funerals. The difficulties and controversies which state medicine has already provoked in some countries also illustrate what happens when hospitals, doctors, and medical techniques are placed under direct governmental control. In North America society applies political regulation to churches and hospitals in only the most general way, and they have both power to manage their own affairs and a distinct and respected status in the community. Clergymen and doctors are relatively independent, for, regardless of what doctrines they preach or techniques they practise, no government office either

[1] I. L. Kandel, *Comparative Education*, p. 215, quoted in *Report of the Royal Commission on Education in Ontario* (Toronto: King's Printer, 1950), pp. 199–200.

directs or advises them. The institutions concerned with the souls and bodies of men thus differ completely from those which deal with their minds.

Why then does society permit such a centralized system in education? The chief reason is that people think it guarantees maximum and equal facilities and opportunities for all children. Officially all schools that follow a given curriculum provide the same facilities. George Smith passed grade twelve at Maple High and Susan Jones did likewise at Central Memorial. They completed the same courses, read the same textbooks, wrote the same examinations, and received the same certificate. In practice, however, is not this similarity an illusion? The character and qualifications of the teachers, the atmosphere of the school, and the attitude of the authorities to children and knowledge may be much better at Maple High than at Central Memorial. One school may regiment its pupils, hand out prepared information, and teach from old examination papers. The other may encourage pupils to assume responsibility and think for themselves, and train them for a competence which will last long after examinations are passed. George's history teacher may have known little history and merely passed on the limited contents of an official textbook. Susan's history teacher may have studied and loved the subject and awakened in his pupils an interest in and understanding of it which will last a lifetime. Two schools whose graduates I regularly teach come to mind; one can be relied upon to give its pupils a sound preparation; the other has a long record of producing students who do well in the school leaving examinations but who fall behind quickly when they go on to higher studies or into employment. In the first, pupils learn to think; in the second, they are merely drilled in memorized routine and taught to regurgitate undigested information for examination purposes. The danger here is, not that pupils get a better education in one school than in another—that is inevitable under any system—but that they, their parents, and educational officials will think they are, or should be, getting the same thing. The system really only serves to disguise rather than discourage inequalities and thus has more weaknesses than advantages.

Yet this sort of inequality can be observed easily in other educational undertakings. Differences among institutions prevail in higher education and are known so to do. No matter what pretensions are made, one university is not as good as another and the B.A. degree received in one place means far more than the same degree conferred by another. Some universities are real universities; some are little more than glorified high schools. Differences in quality are clearly recognized in the commercial world where most people understand the variations among "fancy," "choice," "standard," and "substandard." Schools and courses fall into similar categories, but such a situation is rarely admitted.

One must point also to a danger that tends to become concealed behind the attractiveness of the phrase "equal opportunities." Emphasis on "equal opportunities" tends in practice to become insistence on "the same opportunities," which is a different thing. Standardized curricula, courses, texts, methods, and requirements can ultimately produce the standardized thought, opinion, and habits that result in the mass mind which lives by mass propaganda. Frequent warnings are given that the mass mind constitutes one of the threats to democracy, and many observers have blamed the press, radio, and television as creating it. But surely among the mass media is the centralized programme of schools which forces children into standardized studies in such a way that they soon accept regulation disguised as opportunity. For instance, every child in a province finds on a particular page in a particular book the opinion of one writer who is acceptable to the authorities and what "the book says" is "learned" for an examination. Such a process is an example of a mass medium in its most efficient—and potentially dangerous—form.

The attitude of the Georges and Susans should not be neglected. They need to be impressed with the fact that getting a true education is predominantly a personal process and that no system, method, or requirement can take the place of their own effort and responsibility.

The child needs to attend a school which he regards as a community of which he is a part, and associate with a teacher he respects so as to work and by working learn what he can of the inexhaustible store of knowledge available to him. Instead he goes to a local branch of an impersonal system to receive from a public employee the carefully determined quota of information arranged in prescribed amounts which everyone else is supposed to receive in exactly the same way.

A second reason why the public upholds the centralized public system is its conviction that it keeps all schools *up* to a required standard. One might as well expect a tramp steamer to keep up with the "Queen Mary" in a convoy. For actually the system places schools, teachers, and pupils in an educational convoy in which all must begin together at a given point, keep their allotted positions, proceed at the pace of the slowest, and arrive together at a pre-determined destination. Inevitably it is the weaker schools and teachers that determine the requirements when all follow the same programme. The trend of standards is therefore downward. It is common, for instance, for a school which cannot maintain the general standards to put pressure on the authorities to lower them, and in too many cases the authorities must comply, especially if political expediency requires it. It is common for representatives of weaker schools to sway the opinions of curriculum committees, teachers' conventions, and advisory councils; and always with the plea, not that they cannot do the work, but that prevailing require-ments are too hard for the pupils—an idea that invariably arouses the sympathy of both parents and officials. It then becomes impossible for other schools to keep up their standards. Minimum requirements tend to be the accepted ones because of what one eminent educational official has called "a common misinterpretation of democracy—the fallacy that no one may have what some are unable or unwilling to accept. This fallacy has particular reference to the curriculum."[2]

It is only going a step further to say that the "Queen Mary" has

[2]J. G. Althouse, "Organization of a School System," in *Education for Tomorrow* (Toronto: University of Toronto Press, 1946), p. 32.

no right to go faster than the tramp. A good school may want to secure better teachers, offer extra courses, or add new facilities, but find the improvements impossible to achieve because they cannot be given to other schools at the same time or because other schools can "get along" with less. Slightly different, but just as unfortunate, is the tendency to want to keep up with the academic Joneses. A weak school will very often prefer to add new facilities rather than improve existing ones. Why, for instance, can it not have the privilege of adding two extra high school years so as to do the "same" for its children as another school does? Local groups, and perhaps a politician or two, can always be found to put on the pressure, and, whether or not the change is justifiable, the educational authorities usually find it difficult to resist. The standards are then lowered all around once again; it is always far easier to lower than to raise them. Thus again because of a mistaken interpretation of democracy, a levelling tendency is often directed against the stronger schools. Even in Britain, where there is far more freedom in the schools than in America, the present Prime Minister has warned against those who wanted "nationalization . . . for the public schools—not because the education they give is not good enough, but because it is too good."[3] The diligent preservation of an illusion of sameness at best encourages a dead average and at worst sustains weakness and discourages excellence.

A third factor in the emphasis on centralization is the confused public relations of the schools themselves. Public relations in education are inevitably mixed up with those of governments because the latter have the power and it is to them, not to the schools, that the public must look for leadership. The official viewpoint therefore prevails and, because it is a political viewpoint, it tends to be motivated more by political than educational considerations. The centralized system thus attracts the respect of the public away from the schools, and this very process in turn encourages still more centralization. It may even be that the interests of politicians, trustees, and officials in their own public relations will be incompatible with those of the schools. A minister of education is not

[3]Prime Minister Macmillan in the *Sunday Times*, July 21, 1957.

likely to antagonize a bloc of voters no matter what schools may need or wish to teach; a civil servant will often put his relations with his superiors ahead of his duty to a school; and many a trustee is cautious in supporting or opposing an educational proposal if he needs public goodwill for his own business. The ways which these men have found successful in influencing the public in their own enterprises are not necessarily best suited to the schools.

Moreover, the schools are very often the victims of an old problem of government that the public frequently has too little respect for what it owns and that this respect tends to diminish as interference becomes easy. People respect authority and the schools have none. There is, however, no lack of devices to create public relations for the schools. Courses in teaching methods suggest ways of getting pupils to "enjoy" going to school and numerous subjects are offered to "interest" them. "Education week" extols the virtues of schools; and "Home and School" associations seek to win the support and participation of parents. Yet these devices are artificial, and they have not altered public attitudes towards the schools because other more important elements are needed to create respect.

Responsibility is one important element. No public relations stunts will win the respect for the school of the parent who insists her backward child should grade, the painter who decorates a classroom, or the car dealer who advocates a safe driving course for pupils, if they find the school authorities powerless to say "yes" or "no" without the sanction or interference of a trustee or outside official. No one can make the school look as weak as a trustee or official who plays politics with school contracts, who handles the rental of the school auditorium to community organizations, or who personally takes the initiative in arranging a programme at the school. The school itself must deal with the public if it is to be respected by the public.

The value of a tradition is another, and more subtle, element which almost invariably tends to be ignored in a centralized system. It is difficult to develop respect for a public school when people regard it as they do the water works or electric company—an impersonal utility turning out a commodity or providing a service.

Such an attitude is alien to education. But if a tradition develops around the character of a school, its community respects it and its graduates are inclined to look back with fondness for "the old place," revisit it after they leave, and carry its influence through life. This intangible, but valuable, asset is evident with many private institutions, but it has rarely been successfully cultivated by public schools, whether the huge city high school or the little rural schoolhouse. Consequently, pupils who will later become taxpaying citizens and parents do not have sufficient reason to regard their school, in Cardinal Newman's famous words, as "an Alma Mater knowing her children one by one, not a foundry, or a mint, or a treadmill."

It is surely no exaggeration to say that this absence of respect and lack of tradition are also traceable to the fact that the local schools must often suffer the dullest architecture in town. A few beautiful schools are exceptions, but generally there is much standardization in design and a prevailing fashion for cheap utilitarian construction without character which becomes shabby in a few years. With schools more than with any other institutions it is wise to remember a saying in architectural circles: "man first shapes the house; thereafter the house shapes the man." Unfortunately, however, and perhaps significantly, in the late nineteenth century city schools were built in the same style as county jails, and today most new schools can scarcely be distinguished from factories. It is difficult for pupils, as well as for the public, to feel for a boxy structure with cage-like windows and asphalt or gravelled yards the same warm attachment and respect which are invited by a building with some architectural character of its own and with grassy, tree-bordered playing fields. Expense, location, and other practical considerations must be recognized, but it is hard to recognize the practical when a soft drink company can find a better location and design for its plant than a municipal authority can find for its school, or when the public post office in most communities makes the nearby school look dull and shabby in comparison. Concern for the taxpayer is scarcely an excuse for parsimony in the schools; since he now spends 50 per cent more for liquor and tobacco than for education he seems well able to make a further contribution.

These elements rarely interest the official or trustee. He is concerned with the provision of so many classrooms for so many pupils for so many dollars and he cannot be blamed for emphasizing what, from his point of view, seems to be practical. He is in office for a short time and there is little incentive for him to look ahead twenty or thirty years. He does not have to teach in the school, and the amenities appear to him to be frills. He is not a part of a school itself, so that he is rarely concerned with such intangibles as tradition and school spirit. In one Canadian city the school board included for many years a number of prominent church laymen. In handling the business affairs of their churches, with which they were *directly* associated, they invested wisely in bonds and property, kept the buildings in excellent condition, purchased their organs from the finest makers, were justifiably proud of their stained-glass windows, and insisted on architectural beauty to such an extent that their churches are advertised in tourist literature as sights for visitors to see. They could be business-like, but they could also appreciate tradition and institutional spirit and plan for the future. Yet these same men in their capacity of school trustees associated with no one institution allowed their schools to become ugly, dilapidated fire traps, saved no money and purchased no land, and, when they were forced to build a new school, had to incur an enormous debt and put their building on an inaccessible lot outside the city limits. It need scarcely be added that the building looks exactly like a factory, the income of the teachers is about the same as that of unskilled labour, and the average attendance of parents at Home and School meetings is about 5 per cent.

The public readily accepts this limited outlook of the officials because it is accustomed to accepting their standards and to dealing with them rather than with the schools. Consequently, it allows in the schools conditions which would be considered disgraceful in other institutions and occupations. It grants the right of labour union members to insist on, and even go on strike for, better wages and working conditions. It expects professional men to run their own institutions and practices. It understands tradition in business, religion, and entertainment. It recognizes the advantage of direct control in public affairs. And it is impressed by architectural devices in the construction of its banks, theatres, and grocery stores. But for the schools to seek these things is like Cinderella asking to go to the ball. Small wonder, therefore, that the teaching profession is perpetually awaiting a fairy godmother to deliver it from a kind of community domestic service and give it respect, rights, and returns comparable with those of its sister occupations.

What has just been said would seem to suggest that the role of public opinion in education needs careful examination. Public understanding of the numerous advantages of schools, as well as of their problems, could surely be greatly increased if it were not for the intervention of centralized control. Public interest in education should involve not only the adjustment of the school to the requirements of the people, but also the adjustment of public opinion to the requirements of the school. Indications are that there is too much of the former and not enough of the latter.

The school, because it enters the lives of most members of the community, inevitably receives close attention from public opinion and pressure groups, and, because of its dependence on government, it is most susceptible to their influence. It is a community guinea-pig existing under glass and subject to the will of everyone who wants to do something for, or get something from, education. Every parent hears about classroom incidents; every community organization devises projects for the school; Home and School groups "study" and "discuss" educational matters of all kinds; and every citizen has been to school and "knows" what goes on. When a teacher wears a new dress or is seen smoking a cigarette at recess the fact is related at thirty family dinner tables. Conventions drawing up sets of resolutions will often include some on education. Churches frequently arrange projects in which schools are intimately involved. Ideas of publicity offices or committees designed for schools find their way into the classroom with ease. Unlike the practices of law, medicine, and engineering, and the trades, like plumbing, electrical work, and automobile mechanics, teaching involves no mystery which keeps the public at a respectful distance.

Public opinion is always informative, often sensible, sometimes foolish and generally difficult to determine because it is both obscure and variable. Nevertheless, with all its peculiarities, it should never be ignored, and public enterprises should be both responsible and responsive to it because it is the public's business that is being done. It is this responsibility and responsiveness that make democracy practical, and not the mere fact that the public "owns" an institution. Yet the institution must have some power, not only to encourage the people to respect this object of their attention, but also to enable it in the best interests of all to study public opinion, to distinguish among the many wishes and whims, and then to carry out its proper responsibilities. The dilemma in the public schools is that they cannot serve the public properly because they have not the power to distinguish among the differing segments of public opinion and must cater to too many; they are unable to resist what is mere pressure, and to give some leadership in educational matters. When serving too many masters they are in danger of serving none.

Public opinion is the hardest of all masters to serve and the person or institution that would serve it well must do so directly and have the necessary knowledge and power to control it to a logical extent. In an age of mass production, competitive advertising, give-away programmes, changing fashion, and blatant ballyhoo of numerous kinds, an unprotected institution like a school is about as safe as a babe in a pool of sharks. People who expect free premiums with their cornflakes, who buy books on how to learn to play the piano in half an hour, who will pack a theatre for a crooner and ignore a visiting statesman, who cheer for democracy but will not vote, or who spend restless energy on a whirl of unrelated and unfinished activities, will, for similar reasons, expect showmanship from the schools. In the process of telling and showing others what to do, schools can be forced to adopt, almost without realizing it, a kind of excess motivation which is really little better than smart advertising. Yet schools are responsible, not for selling to, or entertaining, young people, but for assisting in developing their minds, characters, and abilities. They must, therefore, be in a position to concentrate on this task and to put wisdom into their public relations so that the service they can give will be seen to be lasting and worth-while.

Public opinion must be informed if it is to be enlightened, and schools must help form it if they are to be guided by it. Any political party, church, or business firm operates on this principle and from these bodies the public expects and receives leadership. But people will not take seriously the leadership of institutions which cannot speak out and have no power to carry their ideas into effect. Schools must be so deferential to the department, the board, the superintendent, the parents, and, in many instances, to a church and other organizations as well, that leadership within the schools is almost impossible. A vital force is therefore missing in the relations between the schools and the people who own them. Since public officials are even more reluctant than educationists to be frank with the people on educational matters, the public has little opportunity to learn and understand the facts.

Under such conditions, the school presents golden opportunities for meddlers. It must be recognized that often it receives excellent assistance and encouragement from interested individuals and groups, but it must also tolerate interference from excitable social reformers whose enthusiasm is far greater than their common sense. The effect of pressure on the curriculum and on standards, for example, is enormous, and officials and trustees can be all too easily susceptible to them because they do not have to teach the curriculum or enforce the standards. "People who have not been subjected to these pressures and temptations," writes an expert on the subject, "do not realize how strong and how insidious they may be. Things may go well until, say, the daughter of the chairman of the local school board, or of some socially prominent citizen falls below the pass mark. Now, is she far below? Not very far. Are not our standards rather high? Would she not have passed if she attended school in town "X"?

Probably. Was she not unlucky in the examinations? So runs the train of thought; and so are feet set on the slippery slope."[4] The schools are helpless against this pressure.

Even more powerful is the group which interests itself in school matters for its own rather than for the school's ends. The results may be questionable. A profession may need more members or a business or industry more staff, for instance, and because it won't provide appropriate training itself or pay the necessary salaries to attract personnel, it demands special courses in the schools to speed up the output of "trained" workers. Pupils are thereby frequently shifted into qualifying for a job rather than encouraged to secure an educational foundation for several jobs and for life itself. Or a group may urge the teaching of its particular interest, the abolition of a course which it dislikes, the change of a textbook which offends it, or the appointment or dismissal of a teacher for special reasons. The point is, not that various groups should be discouraged from taking an interest, for they may often make valuable and useful suggestions, but rather that schools do not have the power to respond by themselves to what is sensible or to reject what is wrong. Like windmills, they are subject to every passing breeze.

The Home and School Association, for example, is a relatively new and influential organization in educational work. It was first established to provide opportunities for teachers and parents to meet, encouragement of parents' interest in the school and its welfare, and study of educational problems of special concern to both the home and the school. Much good has resulted from the efforts of these societies where these functions are emphasized. Yet the school cannot really speak for itself at Home and School meetings; it can only pass on important suggestions to the authorities. Sometimes the school superintendent is present and does most of the talking. Frequently a few enthusiastic ladies dominate the proceedings and are even able to dominate the school. Projects are occasionally planned to accomplish things which are really the prerogative of the

[4]A. S. Mowat, "High School Examinations," *Journal of Education* (Nova Scotia), June, 1952, p. 4.

staff or board of trustees. Perhaps it is for these very reasons that the attendance is usually small in comparison with the number of parents and the proceedings are often incredibly dull. As agencies of public opinion some of these organizations are, at times, sources of help and encouragement to the schools; others may be at worst groups of over-energetic and ill-informed busy-bodies which are able to hinder the work of the schools because the latter are helpless to discourage interference.

Its indirect operation is the main weakness of public opinion in education. Straining it through politics changes its character and strength. In some instances, the public does not have to impress only schools with its wants but all the officials as well, thus delaying necessary developments. In other instances certain interests, especially those which control votes, use the officials to influence schools in matters which schools alone would be able to resist if they had some power. Either way the schools suffer. Again, there is a sharp contrast with other public institutions and professions which can listen to, negotiate with, or inform public opinion on their own terms.

There is no reason why any section of public opinion, political, denominational, business, or professional, should have, through politics, any more privileges of control over schools than it has over other public institutions. Nor should it have any more right to interpret education to the rest of the people than it has with respect to other activities not its own. If the public wishes medical, spiritual, technical, or legal advice, it goes directly to the appropriate profession and rarely must it seek political or official help or decisions in doing it. If the schools and their teachers were in an equivalent position the impact of public opinion on education and vice versa would be direct and substantial and far more dependable than it is now.

The fact of state control has yet another effect on the operation of the schools: it invites the public to unload all sorts of responsibilities on the schools. People are impressed by the large state system and, as with many social services, they often make the mistake of expecting more from it than it can really provide without their own informed participation and their own contribution of adequate funds. Indeed, the very size of the system actually prevents them from getting familiar enough with it to know their own responsibilities, especially when the necessities of politics force the administration to promise more and more, which is easy and popular, without insisting on the necessary work and money, which is difficult and politically inexpedient. This dependence on the system results in a tendency to identify education exclusively with schooling and to apply the methods of mass production.

Public education is thus an excellent example of the limitations of social services. The government provides the schools, but the schools cannot provide an education; their pupils must get it for themselves. Nevertheless, many people regard schooling as a process which automatically guarantees an "education"—a term they use loosely, which sometimes implies they even expect children to be practically brought up by the school. Officials too are often just as over-confident judging from the elaborate "aims" of education so frequently outlined by them. "To provide," rather than "to get," then becomes the theme and the schools find themselves with far more than they are able to do.

With the convenient general shifting of educational responsibilities to the state, schools are expected to do work for which other agencies, like the home, the church, and the employer, are better fitted. So much attention is being focused on the schools, their methods, and their curricula that many of the excellent opportunities for education which exist outside the schools are being too readily ignored. Four points are important, and are often ignored. First, pupils are not beginners when they start school. They have already been through what are the most formative years of their lives, and they have already learned something of work, truth, love, honesty, and other virtues, as well as gained at least an acquaintance with less desirable traits. Second, during school years they spend only one-eighth of their time in school; the rest is passed with their families and friends, at home or on the streets, asleep, at work, or in play. Third, the teacher is no superman and she cannot act as teacher, parent, clergy-man, doctor, and friend to even one pupil let alone thirty. Fourth, the curriculum taught cannot possibly allow for all the demands of life; the school can give only a general preparation for employment, and much training will have to be secured on the job. Paradoxically enough, therefore, too much dependence on the school weakens education because of the common tendency to place too little emphasis on the seven-eighths of the time children are *not* in school and on the other places where they get a large part of their education.

There are many considerations associated with home and spare time, for instance, which are as important in their effect on the child as anything he does at school, and these are applicable almost universally because they are not really affected by the location of the home or the size of the family income. For example, how much sleep do children get? Unfortunately, bedtime is too late for many growing boys and girls in these days of numerous activities and the popularity of radio and television. One suspects that much of the inattentiveness in class, youthful restlessness, and psychological disturbances of various kinds to which schools are devoting much time, effort, and expense are the results of sheer fatigue. What do children eat? The family oatmeal pot at breakfast is now considered old-fashioned, and Johnny usually must be content with a hurried snack in the mornings. At mid-day he likely follows the current fashion of eating a light lunch so that his whole day at study and at play is spent without substantial nourishment. Then dinner at night is so big by contrast with other meals that he is often too drowsy to do his homework properly. If he has enough money the situation can be made worse by a supplementary diet of soft drinks and candy bars. Indeed, the adequacy of meals nowadays has little to do with family income.

What do children read? The reading problem in the schools has been the subject of much study. But what about the reading problem at home? The ability to read can be acquired, not merely by means of some special methods at school, but also by simple browsing at home. If there are no good books in the house, if no adult member of the family reads or, at least, knows the value of reading, or if opportunities for reading are confined to the comics or big sister's love story magazines, it is ridiculous to expect the school to develop in its pupils a capacity to read. If mother reads aloud too much and does not let the children do it themselves, or if Mother Goose is kept up so long that reading appears childish, or if "good books" are forced on youngsters by overanxious parents, the results can be equally disappointing. Again, opportunity does not depend on family income; the price of a package of cigarettes will buy a good classic or novel, and all the world's literature is available free of charge at the local library.

What kind of conversation do children hear? It is difficult for a school to make a deep impression on a child who hears nothing of any consequence at home. If office gossip and bridge table chatter are the main substance of conversation in Mary's family, similar subjects will be her standard of significance in school and in later life. Family conversation need not be weighty and learned, but simply sensible. A boy can very well learn more about civics from a father who is interested in public affairs or about nature study from a wise farmer father than he will from his teacher, and no course in "homemaking" at school will match a mother's sharing of her experiences with her daughter. Even though a child may learn nothing in detail at home, he absorbs there much of the significance of things and the values of life which the school can tell him about in only an artificial way.

What is home? Regardless of its size and furnishings, do the children think of it as an institution or merely as a shelter? Do they like to be home, or is their headquarters the nearby restaurant or wherever else they expect to find interest and companionship? Some parents seem to regard home merely as a place to hang their hats between parties and meetings, judging from the obvious relation between the time parents spend at home and the number of difficulties in school which their children have. And what is the family outlook on life? Is it a wholesome one of honest interest and service, in whatever field or activity, or is it one of narrow self-interest? What motivates the home will often motivate the child's work at school

What is done with spare time? Young people often learn as much in their spare time as they do in school and at home because there is a wide range of extra-curricular activities through which they may get an education. Summer jobs provide excellent experience, as do hobbies, chores, a paper route, music lessons, cadet training, travel, or simple things like fishing and hiking in the country. And the most worthwhile experience is gained, not by being a social butterfly flitting from one activity to another and doing nothing well, but by concentrating on a few of them and getting the value out of them. Unfortunately, too many people fondly cherish the idea that youngsters are "only young once"; they encourage them to idle away their time doing nothing and some parents are glad to turn the children loose to get them out of the way. Idling, however, can easily become a habit, and laziness and wandering interest in later years frequently result from misuse of spare time in childhood. It is not difficult to prove that young people are happiest, not at endless, aimless play, but at doing something useful. If they can try out their own capabilities early they tend to be better able to decide what they want to do later on. And studies thrive on well-performed outside activities. A large majority of good students are good at other things beside study, while a large majority of poor students are not really good at anything. Which group a boy or girl will be in depends to a large extent on what is done outside of school when he or she is young.

It is a major weakness of the centralized, politically administered educational system that the above questions are not asked often enough when people are not satisfied with the public school. Many parents will demand, and authorities will provide, motivation for the listless, alternative courses for those who are not "interested," and practical training for the "non-academic." Civics must be included to provide the state with "democratic citizens"; religion is needed to help the churches with their work; vocational training is suggested to save the employers time and expense; and everything from "homemaking" to "family living" is added to encourage domestic bliss. No mail order catalogue is more carefully edited than the school curriculum to provide something of everything to please everybody. The unfortunate thing is that many of the students for whom these facilities are provided would be better off with a good sleep each night, a bowl of oatmeal each morning, good books and some companionship and instruction at home, a hobby or two, and several summers of practical experience.

It must be admitted that the school has done and can do much for a child whose home conditions are unsatisfactory. But in such cases it is working under a severe handicap because most teachers have neither the time nor the talent for social service work and because the latter, if emphasized too much, can easily overshadow the regular work of the school. Moreover, the facilities of the school are for this purpose artificial; they can never be what some theorists call "real life situations." School activities are meant to provide a certain amount of life's knowledge which it would be difficult for youngsters to secure without them, but they are based on formal organized programmes. Children read about or are told about things in school, but the greater proportion of their actual experience is gained outside. Most experiences outside the school, because they are natural rather than artificial, make greater impressions on children than what they are told in school. John "takes" citizenship in high school, for example, but what he learns is a highly artificial combination of what a department thinks he should know, an author's opinions, and a teacher's knowledge and experience. Yet if John's father brings him up with the idea that people with different political and religious persuasions are dangerous fools unfortunately a common experience—many school lessons in civics are thereby rendered ineffective. Home life is life itself with its examples and associations, its joy, sorrow, co-operation, frustration, love, and quarrels; and these are far more important in education than anything the school has to offer.

For these reasons overemphasis on the educational facilities of the public schools is scarcely wise. The schools simply have not the status, powers, and personnel required. And even if all schools were efficient and all officials and teachers had the wisdom of Solomon and the showmanship of P. T. Barnum, should they be entrusted with the complete responsibility for teaching all aspects of knowledge and directing every phase of conduct? One has only to think of the control which could be exercised through them by the state. From concentration and centralization of facilities it is only a step to the possible use of the educational system as a propaganda machine, to political control of thought and opinion, to the suppression of differences, and to dictatorship. From this standpoint the general abdication of educational responsibilities by the home, the church, the employer, and other agencies is in the longest view not healthy. To transfer them to schools, which are desperately short anyway of money and personnel seems to be the height of folly.

A second result of over-dependence on the school in a centralized political system might almost be predicted: the appearance of mass production in education. Anyone who attends a sale in a large store knows the problems associated with mass buying and selling—crowds, harassed clerks, bargains for some, sore feet for others, and many indications of the peculiarities of people in the mass. Similar problems are common in the schools which now operate continuously under sale conditions because of the present system of mass education. Accordingly, the schools have had to adopt many of the practices which have proved successful in business in an age of mass supply and demand, especially the technique of mass production. The difficulty is, however, that these practices can be used to control and to sell, but not to educate.

Mass production invariably involves prefabricated parts, standardized styles, specialized methods, continuous and elaborate advertising, and rapid turnover. An efficient assembly line quickly changes a chassis to a finished automobile conforming exactly to specifications, and an accomplished sales staff as quickly passes the product from plant to owner through a maze of selling practices and advertisements. Ask the man who owns one, and you'll find it's the greatest, most exciting, smoothest running car on the market. Drop in to the sales room, request a demonstration, and you'll find it indispensable to your comfort and pleasure. If you haven't the money, a down payment and monthly installments can be arranged. Or is it toothpaste which your dentist "is sure to recommend," or soap which most movie stars use, or the soft drink which the pretty girl in the magazine ad offers for your refreshment? Whatever you wish to buy, you will have at your service a tremendous organization to produce and supply for you and to coax you into making your choice. With such a system, and with variety and competition among products, the manufacturing and business world has given to modern society a fantastic number of goods of all kinds such as the world has never before seen. Because of high costs, production must be efficient; because the consumers are fickle in their tastes, advertising must be blatant, dramatic, and continuous.

Ideas and opinions are distributed in much the same way. Propaganda, in the better sense of the word, is the medium. Political parties and politicians must keep themselves, their platforms, and candidates constantly before the public eye and they maintain huge "machines" to do so. Churches and clergymen cannot be content merely with stating the gospel and their own particular interpretations of it; they must preach and teach, proselytize, and compete, and perhaps exhort and command. Through the whole range of human thought, from the philosopher suggesting a theory to an acquaintance spreading some gossip, people are everywhere being subjected to a mass assault on the mind as great as that on their pocket-books.

The methods used to produce and distribute goods and ideas cannot be used, however, to create and develop talents. One can make a car and sell it to someone. One can develop an idea and convince someone to accept it. But no one has yet sold, or convinced someone to accept, competence in music, an ability to do mathematics, or a knowledge of history. A person may be told of their desirability, or shown how to acquire them, but no facilities or advertising will actually give them to him. He has to develop them himself. Herein lies the difference between mass production and distribution in business and propaganda on the one hand and in education on the other.

Nevertheless, there is a strong tendency to regard the school as an intellectual manufacturing plant admitting raw youngsters, processing them according to curricular blueprints, and turning them into a market in which they are "fitted" for certain specified services. The teacher, in this view, is a technician able to keep the assembly line moving at top speed as well as a trained salesman versed in the methods and jargon which will "sell" his product. It makes a silly picture, but this is in effect the way many officials and parents do view a large, centralized educational system. What they forget is that education involves the development of knowledge, character, and talent which is not facilitated by the usual methods of production and distribution. Put Johnny in at one end: whether an educated man comes out at the other depends largely on Johnny.

Mass education is based on the excellent idea that all should have an opportunity to get as much education as possible. But it has also encouraged an emphasis on mere numbers and a confusion of opportunity with education. It is almost inevitable, therefore, for many people to think that because every child must go to school, every child has the guarantee of an education. And it is almost inevitable for them to expect that, because the state regulates schooling for all, education is a right to be claimed rather than a privilege to be worked for. All this is very hard on the schools which suffer acutely from such exaggerated expectations. Mrs. Jones sends a crippled child to a doctor and she can be told that there is a fifty-fifty chance of a cure; she provides him with music lessons knowing that he may or may not become a competent player or singer. But no such uncertainty is allowed about school. She tends to think that, once her child is exposed to teaching or "covers" a curriculum, he automatically gets an education in proportion to the time he spends. Even if he only makes 50 per cent, he "passes" and is ready for the next stage. The community at large has the same attitude; put all the children in school and the result will be "education for all"; if it isn't, there must be something wrong with the school.

The emphasis today is on numbers. The law requires all children to attend school; the public is expected to provide and pay for the necessary accommodation and instruction; the curriculum is arranged to suit all pupils; the authorities, it is assumed, will find a sufficient number of able teachers; and the pupils will be graded automatically from year to year whether they work or not. If an unacceptable drop-out or failure rate intervenes to upset the arrangement, more money, personnel, facilities, and courses will be devoted to keeping pupils off the streets and off the labour markets. This practice may be wholly sensible and desirable for all pupils in primary grades who must learn how to read, write, calculate, and get certain basic information, but its application to all pupils in senior grades is surely questionable.

The number of years a young person is physically present in school is in itself no indication whatever of the education he gets. Indeed, being in school can actually be harmful to older pupils if they develop habits of sloppy, inaccurate thinking, or dodging responsibilities, or fulfilling requirements with the least possible effort. The provision of electives on a curriculum too often encourages lazy pupils to do a little bit of everything and not enough of anything in particular. The presence of pupils who will not work slows down the pupils who will work. Automatic grading, which is widespread, carries pupils on to levels for which they are not prepared. Standards must inevitably be lowered to meet the average and the greater the number of pupils the lower will be the average. Above all are the simple facts that there are not enough good teachers to handle the numbers, that the presence of poor teachers simply weakens the service provided to *all* pupils, and at the same time that the public will not give teachers the authority, respect, and salaries necessary to provide what it wishes.

Every business man knows the laws of supply and demand and of diminishing returns, but few people recognize that they are as applicable to education as to economics. If the demand for a commodity is great, the facilities and raw materials necessary to produce it must be increased or improved to ensure a supply, and if that is not accomplished either the supply is inadequate or an inferior substitute is provided. The demand for education has expanded enormously with the increase in the population of school age, the raising of the age for compulsory school attendance, the benefits of family allowance, and the fashion which regards going to school as "the thing to do." The supply of education is not automatic, however, for it depends on the number of able teachers and working pupils and on the physical facilities, all of which are almost everywhere in short supply. Consequently, much of the demand for education is not being fulfilled, or mere substitutes for it are being provided. The law of diminishing returns then operates, for the effectiveness of education drops as soon as the school attempts to serve children beyond its real capabilities. The business and professional world has many techniques for meeting these difficulties, but the school has not, and substantial inefficiency is bound to result. It has been pointed out that in the United States in the last eighty years "after adjustments are made for the changed value of the dollar, we find that nine times as much money is spent per year on the education of *each* child and thirteen times as much is invested in the buildings and equipment that each one uses."[5] From both the academic and the business standpoints, this situation is difficult to justify, for the returns to *each* child have not increased in anything like the same proportions.

These problems are aggravated, in large part, by governmental administration which can neither emphasize obligations nor admit weaknesses. Despite artificial attempts to make education popular and learning fun, school can never be an unmarred joy to attend. There is a delayed action to education; it is appreciated when one gets it, but getting it is hard work. Schools, therefore, must always face a negative reaction to their services. But governments cannot permit too many negative reactions among the electorate and to keep the system popular they readily accede to the pressure of numbers and to demands that the schools should be "democratic," "child-centred," and "progressive." These terms are admirable when they are understood, but they too readily become meaningless *clichés* used to cater to those who want the impossible—the privileges of

[5]*New Republic*, January 19, 1953.

education without its obligations. Let Mr. Higgins discuss his lazy, surly son with a teacher and he will usually get frank, sensible advice; let him consult a politician or trustee and it will be easy for him to evoke a "poor dear child" or "something must be done" attitude which will provide satisfaction and less responsibility for him, trouble for the teacher, and some new device to occupy, but not educate, the boy. Because those who determine policy and direct the schools do not have to deal with children, the schools must face this kind of social service outlook on the part of the authorities; it is more attractive in theory than in practice and while it is politically expedient, it is not always educationally wise.

It should be emphasized that these observations apply to *all* pupils. Authorities often justify a general lowering of standards on the assumption that they must "do something" for the average and below-average pupils. Aside from the fact that it is neither sensible nor democratic to cut down opportunities for the able pupils, lowering the standards does not automatically confer educational benefits on the others. The schools have neither the supply of teachers nor the power to train the pupils who perhaps need their services most, and no special courses and options will make up for this lack. Indeed a weaker student may lose whatever ability he might have in a general atmosphere of mediocrity. The reason is, again, political control. Indifferent pupils will not change their ways or be inspired to great effort by the state's benevolence and they will not make progress in weak schools. If, however, the schools themselves had some power to enable teachers to lead and guide these pupils according to their best judgment, the chances are that for them as well as for abler pupils education would be more effective and productive.

It can only be inevitable that the schools are paying enormous penalties by way of criticism and disrespect. The benefits of education, as we have said, are really appreciated by the pupils only after graduation, and the same delayed action is true of the weaknesses, which show up most in after life when schooling proves inadequate to life's challenges. Then the dissatisfied, who have been taught to depend on the school and who have been pushed through with the multitude, look back on school work without respect and feel cheated because they did not get enough out of it. In such cases no politician, trustee, departmental official, or superintendent ever stands forth and takes responsibility for the policy or the weakness concerned; the school and its teachers must take the blame and submit to still further demands from outside which, because of their lack of power and responsibility, the schools cannot possibly fulfil.

The centralized school system today is like a convoy in peacetime. Too many units are proceeding at far less than their capacity and too many are struggling along in a valiant but vain effort to keep up. They are so accustomed to receiving orders from shore that many of them have lost their sense of direction and confine themselves to keeping their places and doing what they are told. Meanwhile the armchair strategists at headquarters do not encounter the elements which the schools must face but rest content as long as everyone keeps together, makes no noise, and shows no lights. Surely the times require something better than this pathetic system. In an age of global warfare, nuclear science, proposed interplanetary communication, and all the complications of modern family and community life, men need knowledge, initiative, vitality, imagination, and judgment. These cannot be developed adequately in a society which forces all its citizens to spend their formative years in regulated routine and restrictive uniformity. And education itself cannot flourish to the extent men need while it is the responsibility of the weakest institutions in the state. It is too important to be directed by a primitive form of administration which other social organizations, including the government itself, have either never tolerated or long since discarded.

5. Teachers as Civil Servants

BY THE TIME POWER IN EDUCATION IS DIVIDED AMONG NUMEROUS politicians, trustees, and officials, little is left for teachers. We have come to accept that fact on the assumption that public interest requires public responsibility and that teachers must therefore be responsible to the state. We might well ask, however, whether their responsibility, which in theory seems obviously in the interest of all concerned with education, has not gone too far; and whether in practice it has not become a position of subservience, which may defeat the purposes of education by killing the teaching profession. The present place of teachers and teaching in the school system does indeed provide justification for concern. An excess of administration at the top means for the teachers the humble status of low-rank civil servants. Emphasis on official opinion and practice exposes teaching to the frustrations of bureaucratic routine. One wonders if the result is not inevitable; certainly it is appalling: the teaching profession boasts more ex-members than any other occupation in modern society. Dominated, it is easily taken for granted, and there may here be a threat to the safety of the democratic state in whose interests the system was begun. "The teaching profession," says Leonard Brockington, "is the first the tyrant seeks to destroy and almost the last the free man seeks to honour."[1]

[1] L. W. Brockington in Robertson Memorial Lecture, Prince of Wales College, 1958.

There is nothing wrong with the act of teaching itself. One of the most important, interesting, and rewarding occupations, it can compare favourably with any other profession. When we ask the reason for the acute shortage and high turnover of teachers we must look, not at the work, but at the conditions of work. Over these conditions teachers themselves have little control; the employer, which is the state, has complete responsibility. It is appropriate, therefore, to examine the effect of the state's responsibility on teaching and on the teachers.

Mark Hopkins's famous description of education should now include an official at the middle of the log, for as earlier chapters have shown the state everywhere comes between teachers and pupils and makes communication between them indirect. Unlike doctors, lawyers, and clergymen—or indeed plumbers, carpenters, and electricians—the teacher is not directly employed by those wishing his services. The real relationship is not between him and his pupils, but between the state and the pupils. The service he performs for them is not something determined by him or his profession but follows a set of requirements laid down by the state. Consequently, Mr. Smith of West Street High is a public employee who teaches any thirty pupils assigned to him by the state in much the same way a government clerk inspects the income tax forms placed on his desk; it will be only their good luck if he should be an able scholar at whose feet young people seek to sit.

This relationship is emphasized on the pupils' side by the compulsion of a state service. Unlike the clients, patients, and customers in other occupations, children are a non-paying captive audience required by law to attend school. Neither they nor their parents are able in the state system to seek out the teachers' services; they are ordered to come and get from them certain services which they may or may not wish, and to take them in the form of a curriculum which the teachers who do the providing are nevertheless not able to prescribe. In business, the value attached to goods or services depends greatly on whether the recipient is offering to purchase or the provider is offering to sell. One of the weaknesses of compulsory state education in a democratic system is that the initiative appears to lie with the provider of the service; the teacher is then something of a local agent only and consequently, pupils and parents do not tend to consider him with sufficient seriousness.

It might be fruitful to examine further how the pursuit of knowledge has been affected by this attitude to knowledge as a commodity to be dispensed rather than something for which the pupils must work.

The teacher always faces the natural resistance to his efforts mentioned in the first chapter the fact that the willingness of people to do what they are asked rarely matches the tendency of others to give advice. Moreover, inertia, as natural in mental life as in the physical world, must be overcome by the teacher in his pupils before anything significant can be taught by him and learned by them. Unlike other workers, therefore, the teacher can never assume that his clients really want his services or that they are willing to make the required effort to take full advantage of them. Unfortunately also he cannot assure them of tangible services which will be of immediate benefit. When a contractor builds a house the results are visible and the direct consequence of action by the performer of the service which the owner requests and pays for. Nothing quite so obvious follows from teaching a course in history or algebra: the effects on the mind are not immediately apparent and, indeed, there may be no effects at all if there is insufficient effort on the part of the pupil. In education the customer is never sure of what he wants or what he is going to get, although it is the customer who must exert the main effort. This situation makes education impossible to guarantee, difficult to predict, and hard to understand and appreciate.

It is this particular aspect of education which helps to make it so incompatible with direct governmental administration. When people look to government for action and benefits they tend to expect service that is immediate, tangible, and practical: they count on the government to do what is necessary and produce obvious results. Politicians and civil servants, in turn, because of their need for popular support and of the very nature of their occupations wish to offer the same sort of services, and they too want to see direct action and visible results. Education they are apt to interpret as a political service rather than as an essentially human process. The teacher caught between public and administration, has the greatest difficulty in emphasizing that learning is not a commodity to be thus demanded and dispensed and that the final results depend largely on the pupils.

The dominance of the official attitude thus tends to place education among the social services which are expected to be handed out automatically. Like pensions which come with old age or sickness, like family allowances which are paid out from birth, school certificates are regarded by many as the right of pupils who reach a certain age. Actually, the opportunity for education is the social service; education itself cannot be an automatic right because no one is able to give it. This distinction is vital: if it is not made it becomes impossible to maintain the standards and carry out the responsibilities involved. It is difficult, however, for the state to make this distinction. Its control is so embracing and detailed that it is easy for it to assume, and the public encourages it to assume, that it is giving the education, not just the opportunity. It is then only a short step to an emphasis on the state's *giving* rather than the pupils' *getting*, and the consequent dilution of standards and responsibilities in the interest of "education for all."

The social service outlook inevitably affects the teachers and their work by making it difficult for the public to appreciate the teaching profession and understand its problems. The state, the public, and the pupils are not encouraged to regard teachers as leaders and guides in their fields directing and assisting pupils in their quest for knowledge. Indeed, it is hard for teachers to think of themselves in this role. Since they are expected rather to be dispensers and coaches, their qualifications and achievements tend to become secondary in official and public eyes. So long as there are enough of them to "fill the schools" and expose every boy and girl to some kind of instruction, the state is too easily satisfied and little is done to improve the status of the profession. Under these circumstances the problems of salary, working conditions, training, and supply inevitably appear, and as inevitably remain.

So much has been said about the low level of teachers' salaries that in most places it is taken almost for granted by the public, and considered by officials as being like the weather in that nothing much can be done about it. There is simply not enough recognition of the fact that any good teacher can be lured out of his job by business firms, unless his devotion to teaching is greater than his desire to improve his standard of living, and that the effectiveness of public education declines with every resignation. Admittedly there has always been a tendency for people to underrate the value of culture and to underpay preachers, teachers, and artists, and, as far as teachers are concerned, this tendency is strengthened by the public's attitude that somehow the government should pay less than other employers. There is little to counteract the tendency: if a good teacher resigns and there is no equivalent replacement, a permit or temporary licence can easily be issued to a less competent person so that the job will be filled. The prospect of reform with respect to salary is remote so long as such a practice is possible.

The conditions under which teachers work are, however, a far more serious problem than salaries. The profession is, as has been noted, run like a civil service despite the fact already emphasized that teaching bears no similarity whatever to the functions for which civil service administration is designed.

The classification system illustrates the problem. It is the governmental practice of standardizing and classifying positions and qualifications which has been applied to the teaching profession, so that each teacher is put in a category and appropriately labelled. There are many grades from "superior" to "permit," each divided into classes alphabetically or numerically. Appraisal of this system would involve "merit rating," and this teachers' organizations seem to fear. Now classification may work in the routine of the civil service where it is by and large functions rather than individuals which are classified, but can this arrangement be efficient in teaching where the individual himself is, or should be, paramount? Surely it is no more sensible than it would be to divide doctors, lawyers, clergymen, politicians, and others into first, second, and third class, as well as "temporary" and "permit." The knowledge, methods, and character of teachers simply do not allow them to be standardized and classified without weakening teaching as a whole by subsidizing the incompetent and holding back and discouraging the able. One graduate with a B.A. or one "second class" teacher is not the same as another bearing the same label. A course taught by one teacher is not in effect the same as that taught by another, and no official text, course of study, or regulation will make it so. Mathematics teachers, who are scarce, cannot be classified in the same manner as English teachers who are comparatively plentiful; but the law of supply and demand has not been allowed to operate in education. Indeed, the classification system is one of the chief reasons why good teachers leave, why poor teachers remain, and why the profession is so powerless. "All for one and one for all" is an excellent tactic in its place, but is education necessarily the place for the traditional procedure of convoys that it is the slowest which set the pace?

The practical difficulties which lead to reliance on this classification system are the size of the whole organization and the remoteness of the employer. Teachers do not form a small, closely knit profession with a special and distinct place in the community, but are rather an enormous group with limited association among its members. There are more school teachers in Canada than doctors, lawyers, nurses, engineers, and clergymen combined, and, because the administration of their activities is so centralized, it is difficult, under political control, to accord them the privileges of professional recognition rather than just those of the holding of a job. It is also difficult to recognize ability. Because the minister of education and his departmental officials and the members and staffs of school boards have no real contact with a school, they have no sure way of making an official distinction between the teaching ability and professional reputation of Mr. Black and Mr. Brown. They may pay and promote on seniority only. They may favour the academic politician who is popular and knows the right people. They may judge a teacher by the number of committees he sits on or extracurricular activities in which he joins. They may classify on diplomas secured and summer courses attended. They may favour "professional" study in method-ology, organization, or administration. What they are almost com-pletely incapable of recognizing and rewarding officially is initial knowledge of the subjects to be taught, renewed or maintained com-petence in these subjects, natural ability to teach and productive relations with pupils. The tradition of the classification thus continues strong and, consequently, there is not sufficient reward for the out-standing, incentive to the mediocre, or check on the incompetent.

It would seem that the attainments of pupils would be a particu-larly revealing means of assessing teachers. But officials have virtually no regular contact with all varieties of school children, and tend to regard them in anything but realistic ways. They often look upon all children as benefiting greatly, perhaps even equally, from their mere presence in school, regardless of the type of teaching they receive or the amount of work they do. They usually regard the completion of a grade or course as bringing a given number of pupils to the same level of attainment. Consequently, mere exposure to teaching and the "passing" of examinations, even at only the 50 per cent level, are magnified out of all proportion to their true significance. Attendance and movement from one grade to another, may tell little about either the pupil or the quality of the instruction he has received, but under the circumstances of the centralized system they count for much and the calibre of the teachers is too easily overlooked.

The classification system combines with the social service outlook to subordinate the qualities of the individual teacher to the arrange-ment and appearance of the organization. An able science instructor may leave a school and be succeeded by a mediocre one, or a history teacher may lose touch with his subject; no change is apparent as far as the course, the curriculum, or the certificate are concerned, but the essential difference lies where it is most important, but least obvious, in the teaching. With the individual thus subordinated to the job, it is to be expected that the ablest teachers would become discouraged: they may not be paid more than others in the same classification and they may not teach beyond the limits of the official requirements.

Teaching is weakened further by the official necessity of making the system "look good" to the voters. The authorities, who must at all cost retain popular support, are sensitive to failure rates in general and to the adverse fortunes of their constituents' children in particular. They will seek remedies, not in emphasizing that pupils must work—such frankness would be dangerous to the popularity of elected officials—but rather in tinkering with the schools and the curricula. Official interference with teaching standards and practices is common, not so much on behalf of the pupils as because of the need for the vast educational system to show favourable results. This emphasis on the machine rather than on the school adds greatly to the teachers' work. It is virtually impossible, for instance, for them to get the lazy to work if the pupils know that automatic grading is the official policy; and it is hard to convince some parents that what their children will get from school will actually depend far less on the grade reached or the courses "passed" than on the ambition they have, the attention they pay, and the work they do. Officials will not, indeed under the circumstances they cannot, enlighten the pupils or parents by admitting weaknesses. An examination of the annual reports of departments of education reveals the dullest of government documents; they omit everything that might indicate weaknesses and emphasize everything that shows the magnitude of the system and the numbers participating in it.

Of all the results of centralized state control for the practice of teaching, the most powerful, and at the same time, depressing, is the conformity it requires. Teachers must always follow someone else's rules, carry out other peoples' projects, and depend on persons outside the profession for initiative, judgment, and leadership. A good teacher who loves his subject, his pupils, and his profession would like to do justice to all three, but he must follow the course of study and the assigned textbook, teach no more than what is required, and prepare for examinations set by remote personnel. His work and his method are all laid down in detailed regulations and there is little scope for individual initiative or professional leadership. Power and imagination in teaching are always in danger of being interfered with by those who control the school system. The prevailing official attitude seems to be that somehow the teacher and his profession must be regulated and watched lest either might say something wrong or do something unofficial, and that somehow each school and its work must conform to every other school and its work. The result is inefficiency in a profession where individual ability and character are most important. "A pall is cast over the classrooms," said Justices Black and Douglas in the United States Supreme Court when discussing what happens when teachers are watched too closely.

There can be no real academic freedom in that environment. . . . there can be no exercise of the free intellect. Supineness and dogmatism take the place of enquiry. A "party line" lays hold. It is the "party line" of the orthodox view, of the conventional thought, of the accepted approach. . . . The teacher is no longer a stimulant to adventurous thinking; she becomes instead a pipeline for safe and sound information. A deadening dogma takes the place of free enquiry. Instruction tends to become sterile; pursuit of knowledge is discouraged. . . . A school system producing students trained as robots threatens to rob a generation of the versatility that has been perhaps our greatest distinction.[2]

The pressure for conformity has yet another unfortunate effect in that it encourages the kind of person who enjoys conforming and who learns how to do it well in a system in which response to political influence is acceptable. The result is an illustration of what Sir Edward Beatty called the chief weakness of public enterprise: the tendency of many public employees to play politics rather than to do their work with full efficiency. Teachers are so dependent on government officials in a system where their worth is indicated by their place in the classification and by "credits" rather than proven by their work, that many of them are often forced to adopt political methods to secure appointment, recognition, and promotion. When actually teaching, they can too easily subordinate their own thinking and efforts to the kind of window dressing which impresses officials and thereby stifle that innate quality of initiative and independence

[2]*Adler* v. *Board of Education*, 342 U.S. (1951) 485.

necessary to scholarship. The welfare of schools and the good name of the profession are always damaged by such tactics, and an unfair advantage is taken of teachers who are independent in outlook, who attend to their work, and who have no time or inclination for personal politics.

There is no escaping the fact, however, that in most professions it is often the nonconformist who does the best work. Many of the ablest politicians and businessmen are "characters," and it is often just this fact that makes them successful. Anyone looking back on his school days will remember that some of his best teachers were "different," and, indeed, that they were not always popular. Nevertheless, there is a strong tendency in school administration to distrust difference and ability in favour of sameness and mediocrity. Practically every critic of current educational policy has emphasized the point and given illustrations. From personal experience I can confirm their observations, for, of the official criticisms I have heard of schools and teachers, by far the most numerous have been directed against the better ones and the different ones. Let any two parents test the system by complaining to an official, one to the effect that Miss Smith's standards are too high, and the other to the effect that Miss Jones' standards are too low. The chances are overwhelmingly in favour of Miss Smith getting the official reprimand and Miss Jones going on unhindered.

The mediocrity which the pressure for conformity always encourages is responsible for a remarkable paradox in education, the presence of anti-intellectualism in the very place where it should have no place—the schools. Ill-prepared teachers and indifferent pupils are, of course, prone to excuse their shortcomings by scoffing at those who express ambitions and display exceptional talents. But this attitude is more widely encouraged by the combination of political allegiance and the suppression of individualism which operates for the profession as a whole.

The prevailing attitude is one of the main reasons for the drop-outs from the teaching profession, and for the fact that while young people see more of teaching than they do of any other profession so few of them want to teach. There are numerous rewarding features of teaching and many teachers secure these either because they find a way of not minding the system or are protected from it by discerning principals. "But," wrote a president of the Canadian Teachers' Federation, "the restrictive atmosphere in a host of trivial matters often turns competent and self-respecting individuals from the profession. The educator needs both security and freedom—security from the open and subtle pressures of the community and freedom to be an individual or even a 'character'. . . .Denial of full political freedom makes a second-rate citizen. Limitation of personal freedom makes a teacher a race apart [*sic*]. Where such conditions exist is it any wonder that the profession is avoided like the plague?"[3] Few people outside the profession understand this situation. Certainly few would tolerate it in any other occupation.

Nowhere are the effects of state control of teachers more obvious than in their training. We should, therefore, examine the governmental administration of teacher training and its effect on the standards of admission, the quality of the courses, and the methods of licensing.

It will be remembered that teaching is the only profession or occupation in which the state controls the training and licensing. In law, medicine, theology, and the like the requirements are set and administered jointly by a university and the professional organization concerned, and the licence is given by the profession after certification by the university. In the trades, apprenticeship and occupational recognition are largely in the hands of an appropriate association. The government has little or no part in these fields even where prospective civil servants are involved. The teacher's licence however is a state permit, not a professional diploma.

This licence is the chief instrument of the state's control. The department of education lays down the requirements which must be met for it and issues it. These requirements will naturally set the standard for all teacher training, and those who train teachers or plan to teach will be guided by them. This process ensures that all teachers

[3]L. John Prior in the *Educational Review* (N.B.) Sept.–Oct., 1954.

will look to the government for guidance and leadership, for whoever controls the entrance to a profession effectively controls the profession.

Control is also exercised directly through the normal schools and university departments of "education." The normal schools are owned by the government and administered by its officials. Their policy and standards are, therefore, the direct responsibility of politicians and civil servants. Control over the university departments is more subtle, but none the less powerful. Their graduates must be recognized and licensed so that professors of "education" have to fulfil the official requirements of provincial departments of education rather than of university senates. "They are almost inevitably compelled," said a president of the Canadian Teachers' Federation, "to accept the expedient dictates of those departments as to entrance standards, length of training, and nature of certification. They are also beholden, directly or indirectly, to those government departments for their finances and for their staffing even though they may be ostensible faculties of universities."[4]

The role of the teaching profession itself in the process of training its future members is usually incidental, at best secondary. Representation on an advisory committee or licensing board is about the most it can expect, in contrast to the dominant role played by other professions in their own fields. The significant fact is that the profession can lay down no regulations or issue no certificate *of its own*. It therefore lacks the power to impress its wishes on government, training institutions, and prospective teachers.

This arrangement might be acceptable if the government were a satisfactory authority to train and license teachers. One wonders, however, what special qualifications politicians and civil servants have in respect to teaching which apparently have not been recognized in other fields, and whether their qualifications are better than those of the universities and the teaching profession. Yet the deciding factor is actually not one of qualification but of political necessity. Once the state assumes a direct and comprehensive administration of

[4]George L. Roberts, quoted in *Halifax Chronicle Herald*, June 11, 1958.

the school system it is forced to train and license the teachers *to maintain the system*. The ranks must be filled, and filled with people who are prepared to work in the system with sympathy for its aims and with respect for its regulations. On reflection, one might even be moved to suggest that the filling of the ranks and administration are now such major problems that maintaining the system is a greater determinant in training and licensing than is the teaching of pupils.

The general standards and the outlook of normal schools and university departments of "education" are inevitably affected by the attitude of the state in these matters. Training institutions in other fields must look to university authorities, various allied university disciplines, professional associations, and particularly to employers who are fussy about whom they hire. But teacher training institutions look to the government, which knows little about teaching and which will in the end hire all candidates for licences. Because the government must somehow fill the schools, it has been thought necessary to provide entrance to the profession at several levels, and most of these are low. Candidates, for instance, can enter on a "permit" with no official qualifications, or on a "temporary" licence with partial qualifications. The training institutions thus have no very high standards to meet and are encouraged to be lenient in their own requirements. We, therefore, find, as a direct result of state influence, soft attitudes in every phase of teacher training.

Such attitudes are obvious in the standards of admission to teacher training. Candidates can enter normal schools after the completion of high school or, in many places, before completing high school. They can enter some university departments of education at the undergraduate level and get various grades of licences depending on the number of years spent there. Other such departments are entered after the completion of a bachelor's degree. Moreover, seemingly to make sure that the bottom of the barrel is properly scraped, the authorities provide endless ways of meeting requirements at all levels by taking short courses. Although many good candidates qualify by serious and prolonged study, the inevitable happens under such an arrangement: prospective teachers too often take the line of least resistance and enter the profession by the easiest means, encouraged by employing officials and trustees who have urgent demands for teachers to fill and who do not in any case pay enough to make the advanced work worth while. The prevailing level of qualification is indicated by the fact that the average total number of years of both schooling and training completed by Canada's teachers is approximately thirteen.[5]

The vast proportion of teacher training students therefore enter normal school at the age of seventeen or eighteen and emerge to teach a year later. Their limited knowledge and experience, for which all other professions and many occupations have as yet no place, are thus deemed by the state to be sufficient for teaching. Moreover the general quality in any given year is further governed by three factors: the supply of teachers, which, if low, usually loosens the requirements; the salary and working conditions, which, if unattractive, usually discourage those who seek careers rather than jobs; and the competition from other occupations, which, if stiff, is hard for normal schools to meet. Because these qualifications all apply at the present time, the calibre of students attracted to normal schools is, on the whole, comparatively low. By and large normal schools receive what is left over after the universities and employers have taken the top students from the high schools. In New Brunswick, for example, of the 568 students enrolled at Teachers' College in 1958-9, only 8 per cent had first class standing on leaving school and less than 22 per cent would qualify for entrance to university![6] Despite what may be said about teacher training being professional in nature, it is difficult to consider professional the work arranged for students of this age and calibre.

The usual teacher training course itself does not go very far to counteract this lowering tendency; indeed it might be considered as big a cause of the teacher shortage as low salaries and unattractive working conditions. The chief characteristic of the course is likely to be the fact that it is given at or below the level of the students who

[5]M. E. LaZerte, *Alberta Teachers' Association Magazine*, October, 1954.
[6]*Educational Review* (N.B.) Nov.-Dec., 1958, p. 18.

take it. Courses in methods, child psychology, and the like, which look well on the official course of study, can be, at the level they are given, little more than the playing of games, the making of scrapbooks, the compiling of notes, the hasty learning of a few simple rules on how to impress a class, and the acquiring of some snatches of information about school law, the prescribed texts, and the official curriculum. There is no time for adequate study of the subjects to be taught in the schools, even for those who enter the training with poor records. Nor is there opportunity for sufficient reading and discussion in any field of knowledge in order to get some acquaintance with life, people, and affairs before setting out to lead and instruct children. The course is simple and dull for bright students, who find it no challenge whatever; it is tragically misleading for weak students, who are deluded into thinking that what they are getting is in any way an education. The requirements of the course are the most formidable evidence of its calibre: the failure rate is usually negligible even among students with the poorest high school records. Even those who fail can often get some kind of licence, and this fact lowers still further the standards of the profession and the incentive to work. In the New Brunswick institution mentioned above, and despite its obviously low standards of admittance only two of 400 in the class of 1958 were refused a licence![7] Good students, who will be expected to show some ability and to work in other courses, are quick to notice these facts, with the result that the normal school is widely regarded among them as an academic poor-house. It is ironic, yet tragic, that of all the facilities in all parts of the educational system, teacher training is by far the easiest and weakest.

One of the proper functions of normal schools is to provide instruction in how to teach subjects and how to handle children. Some helpful suggestions are given, but the prevailing concentration on methods in the normal schools is, in too many instances, really little more than instruction in how to camouflage weakness. The simple fact is that students cannot learn how to teach if they don't know what they are teaching, and most of the students have poor back-

[7] *Ibid.*

grounds in their school subjects. The state may as logically run a medical school and try to turn out doctors by giving courses in bedside manner to first-aid workers. The public may wonder, and industry and business may complain, about the shortage of mathematicians and the inability of the average employee to do simple mathematical problems. The reason is not hard to find: "Although all states," reports the Carnegie Corporation, "require *education* courses for secondary mathematics teachers, a third of the states require no *mathematics* for certification of math teachers. At the elementary level the situation is even worse. In the majority of instances a prospective elementary school teacher can enter a teachers' college without any credits in secondary school math."[8] The result is poor instruction in the schools and a steady increase in the number of pupils who either fail mathematics or do not take it at all. This situation is regrettably common in all subjects.

The results of this type of training are seen not only in poor instruction but also in the reducing of requirements and the lowering of standards in the schools. It is very common for teachers who are not adept at mathematics themselves to say that mathematics is not "important" to children in "everyday life" and thus rid themselves of an unwanted teaching burden and deprive their pupils of valuable training. Language requirements, both ancient and modern, are everywhere being dropped from the curriculum, not so much because pupils do not need them as because teachers cannot teach them. Pupils are not being encouraged to read by teachers who themselves are not in the habit of reading. When it comes to standards, a teacher can judge the accomplishments of children only if she is herself sufficiently accomplished. She cannot mark essays, indeed she probably will not assign them, if she cannot write herself or if she does not know a well-written piece of prose when she reads one. She will accept sloppy, inaccurate classwork and homework if she is careless, and she will see nothing wrong with laziness and inattentiveness on the part of her pupils if she is not sufficiently interested in her own work. The authorities cannot expect too much of weak teachers

[8]Carnegie Corporation of New York, *Quarterly Report* (Jan., 1956).

because of the shortage and the curriculum will be trimmed accordingly. Parents in turn will be lulled by high marks and automatic grading into accepting the standards expected, and their children, who will not be likely to do more in school than they have to, will take what they get and be satisfied. Is it really too harsh to say that so many weaknesses begin in the governments' normal schools that they are like printing presses issuing counterfeit money which circulates unsuspected from hand to hand until it debases the national currency?

A similar situation exists in many university faculties of education, even those which require a B.A. for entrance. The standards of admission and achievement are usually far lower than those of other graduate faculties or of the professional schools, and a general opinion prevails among students that the "education" course is the easiest to get into and get out of. It is reported that of the college freshmen in the United States, who took the draft-deferment tests, the majority in each professional classification passed; the exception was students in "education," of whom only a quarter passed. The Educational Testing Service, which administers college entrance tests has reported that "education" students have the poorest records of all those who attend colleges and universities.[9] There are similar weaknesses in Canadian institutions, and they are further perpetuated by the fact that American standards are also widely accepted here, because, as the Massey Commission has pointed out, the senior personnel in Canadian schools and training institutions "almost automatically make their pilgrimage" to American teachers' colleges and "our lazy, even abject, imitation of them has caused an uncritical acceptance of ideas and assumptions which are alien to our tradition."[10]

Aggravating the situation is the existence of the same variety of short cuts encountered in the normal schools. All other professional college courses require attendance at full sessions and the completion of regular requirements. But "education" students can usually take

[9]*New York Times*, Feb. 1, 1953.
[10]*Report of the Royal Commission on National Development in the Arts, Letters, and Sciences* (Ottawa: King's Printer, 1951), p. 15.

short courses, special courses, summer courses, correspondence courses; and the waiving of regular requirements is common. In many instances the standards asked of students taking these courses are far below those required of regular students, and the associations involved are a poor substitute for sustained contact with other students in regular session. This fact is not sufficiently recognized because a degree or certificate obtained by short-cut credits is not distinguishable from the regular one. Yet the mere existence of these short cuts reduces the prestige and significance of the regular programme itself.

The state's influence in training becomes complete at the level of graduate study in "education." At this level are trained the directors of the school system: the administrators, superintendents, and specialists who become employed in government departments of education, school board offices, and teacher training institutions. At this level, therefore, future policy for the schools is greatly affected for it is the personalities, training, and outlooks of these people which are the background for the theories, methods, texts, and regulations to be established in the schools. Moreover, teachers looking for pro- motion are directed towards this training because for them it usually has official favour over all other post-graduate work. Inevitably, therefore, the political and official outlook of the hierarchy of the school system creeps into and indeed prevails in graduate work. Courses then become directed towards administration and mechanics with emphasis on selling a social service. There is scarcely room for subjects which encourage scholarship in a programme with this direction and it soon gets pushed out of attention in favour of techniques.

An examination of some of the features of this kind of training will bear out this description easily. Graduate courses in "education" under the present system have to be at a much lower level than those in other graduate departments. This is inevitable since many of their students are drawn from the weak undergraduate programmes in "education," and the work must be designed accordingly. Other students come from a wide variety of honour and pass undergraduate courses, and the requirements therefore must be worked out on the basis of some common denominator to suit all of them. Furthermore, the courses in techniques and administration could scarcely be "advanced" study; not only must they be elementary because the background of knowledge required is limited, but they must also be practical because the jobs to which many of those who take them aspire require of them not so much intellectual leadership as an interest in administration. The difficulty of ensuring proper academic content can be illustrated by the courses in "the history of education," "the philosophy of education," and "the psychology of education" given for postgraduate credit. Unfortunately students in "education" rarely have a sufficient grounding in history, philosophy, and psychology on which to base graduate study. The results can be unfortunate, and can be seen in, for example, the influence of people who take "the psychology of education" far too seriously considering their limited experience of the discipline of psychology itself.

An emphasis on method and administration is everywhere obvious at this level of training. Courses in them are proliferated and expanded out of all proportion to their real significance and then splintered and expanded again to such an extent that entire courses are devoted to minor aspects of a subject or procedure which could readily be grasped after a little reading. The calendars of many schools of "education" usually make those of other professional schools look meagre in comparison. Teachers College, Columbia, the Mecca of so many "educators," offers no less than 800 courses. The University of Alberta offers eleven courses in educational administration alone, including one on the administration of the guidance programme and two especially for students in physical education. Evidently these are not exhaustive, for a special course occupies senior students with the mysteries of "school buildings and pupil transportation"[11] and includes instruction in such vital subjects as "Operation, utilization and maintenance of the school plant. Evolution of pupil transportation. Planning bus routes. The driver and his

[11]"Education 568."

duties. Bus standards." A footnote in the calendar emphasizes that the course is "normally restricted to graduate students"—perhaps to discourage janitors and bus drivers from applying for it. It is difficult to avoid the conclusion from this and similar evidence in most teacher training calendars that "education" is the best example of the modern tendency to learn more and more about less and less. Unfortunately, however, inflated trivia sound impressive to politicians and trustees who hire and promote teachers, and who cannot always consider the relationship of the courses taken to the actual teaching to be done. For instance, one can teach history on credentials earned in physical education—a peculiar transfer of benefit which makes the whole programme dangerous. Again the familiar conclusion is unavoidable; courses in "education" do not make teachers as much as recruits for a system dominated by its administration.

Graduate degrees usually involve the writing of a thesis. There has been substantial criticism of both the topics and the quality of theses in "education." This study is not the place for a detailed discussion of theses, but I can myself support the criticism from my reading of numerous appallingly bad ones and I have come to the strongly held conclusion that in many places the requirements for pedagogical theses should have more supervision from faculties of graduate studies and other university departments than departments of "education" are now inclined to permit. Two points are relevant to this discussion. I have noted that theses in "education" bear a marked similarity to government documents in style, theme, and methods of gathering data and reaching conclusions. Certainly they bear no resemblance to research studies in other areas of investigation. Surveys, questionnaires and tables, and descriptions of techniques, procedures, and methods expressed in the official jargon of administration betray the dedication of graduate study to the office and the system rather than the classroom. This dedication is also encouraged by the graduate student's lack of sufficient training in some academic discipline to enable him to do real research as distinct from description of techniques. The second point relevant to theses reinforces the first. Few theses make any real contribution either to the teaching abilities of the candidates or to the literature of the profession. Few are published to be read by teachers; few convince any teachers who happen to read them. An instance is taken here from the United States, but there are many analogies in Canada; thousands of studies have been made on the teaching of mathematics, 1,400 in the teaching of arithmetic alone up to 1946, yet says the Secretary of the Educational Testing Service, "we still know little of a definitive nature about how mathematics should be taught."[12]

A qualification must be emphasized. Much depends on the normal school or university department of education at which candidates for the teaching profession are trained. A few teachers and professors of "education" are excellent scholars and teachers with wide knowledge of children and of schools. These people can be depended upon to give sound training; the pity is that they have not more independence of politics and better material to work with. Many of them are fully aware of the weaknesses of teacher training and would do something about them if they could. Unfortunately there are other instructors in "education" who are quite incapable of training teachers, and they are to be found especially in normal schools where the salaries of staff are low and opportunities for advancement limited and in university departments of "education" where the staff is cut off from regular academic and professional control. Some are poorly trained themselves; some cannot teach; some know little about either schools or children and live in ivory towers of theory; some have little respect for knowledge or what they call "subject matter areas," and put almost exclusive emphasis on techniques. The many weaknesses in the teaching of teaching remind one of the question: "If the salt has lost its savour, wherewith shall it be salted?"

Despite these limitations of state-controlled training, attempts to change it or get around it and enter the profession through other channels, such as graduate study in regular academic subjects, are frustrated by the rigid exclusiveness of the system. The administrative hierarchy clings to its monopoly and carefully fosters the

---

[12]Educational Testing Service, *Annual Report*, 1954-5, p. 28.

impression that anyone who takes a normal school or university "education" course is therefore a qualified teacher. The common practice of licensing even the few failures in these institutions carries this tactic to a fantastic extreme. This impression inevitably leads to another, that no one can become a teacher who has not taken such a course. Thus the state contributes in still another way to the shortage of teachers by erecting a barrier to many able students who simply will not take teacher training because when they hear of its quality they consider it a waste of time.

One reason for this remarkable situation is the perhaps natural tendency of administrative personnel to be suspicious of academic competence, a tendency unchecked in "education" by the kind of opinion and influence exercised in other fields by university and professional authorities. Techniques are bound to displace learning as determinants in a system run on civil service lines, geared to the pace of the average, and staffed with great difficulty. The man with a few handy methods, or, worse, *the* method, at his disposal, fits in; he will follow the regulations, speak the jargon, and teach the pre-scribed texts. The well-trained scholar may be at a disadvantage; his standards may be high; he may be independent in his thinking; he will know more than the textbooks. In short, he is difficult to fit into a system; he belongs rather to a profession, and to a profession, not the school system, he is encouraged to go.

The emphasis in the current arrangements for teacher training is usually excused on the ground that all good scholars do not auto-matically become good teachers. This is true, just as true as the fact that all teacher trainees do not automatically become good teachers. A good combination of scholarship and method of presentation is, of course, most desirable; it is also not common. Yet there is certainly no reason why methods should be favoured over scholarship: the glib talker who can "teach" but doesn't know what he is "teaching" is far more dangerous than the one who knows but who teaches with difficulty. Most good scholars do become good teachers for the simple reason that they know their subjects, they may have studied under able teachers, they know from first-hand experience what the learning process is about, and they have enough common sense to pick up techniques in a relatively short time. Certainly they would seem to be better prospects, especially for high school teaching, than weak students who have only teacher training and lack other qualifications. Because the opportunities for scholars who have not had teacher training are few in the school system and numerous outside, general comparisons are difficult to make. I have watched both types at work in my own and in other institutions. The teacher training graduates are usually better prepared for teaching during the first month or two in the classroom because they have been taught some schoolroom procedure. But they find, or rather their pupils later find, that adeptness at procedure is no substitute for knowledge; and in too many cases superficial entertaining and emphasis on textbooks and projects become the established routine. Too often analysis of methods is neglected in favour of slavishly following *the* method which was learned in teacher training; discussion in class is often confined to the posing and answering of stereotyped, standardized questions; and the kindling of the imagination of the pupils is abandoned in favour of prepared stimuli and the expected response. The results which I have witnessed confirm a statement of the late Canon A. S. Walker, President of Kings' College: "Guidance," he said, "is one thing. Control of thought is entirely another, and modern method tends too much to the latter concept of what teaching ought to be and do."[13] On the other hand, most of the scholars who have been employed without teacher training soon overcome an initial awkwardness, learn from experience, catch on to the details of procedure quickly, or seek the advice of colleagues, as everyone else must do in any job. They teach on the basis of their substantial knowledge and abilities, and their judgment and imagination is rarely hampered by excess routine. Unquestionably the best high school teaching I have seen has been done by able honour graduates in regular academic subjects who have never been near a teacher training college yet who know what they are doing because they know what they are saying.

[13]A. S. Walker, "Trends," *Canadian Education*, Dec., 1953, p. 39.

Immediately important questions arise. Why not combine good scholarship with teacher training? Would not a good scholar be a better teacher if he had teacher training? As the final chapter will indicate, I believe that teacher training is essential but it must really be training and it must be provided under the right auspices and the right conditions. Unfortunately, the teacher training given today is below the level of the good scholar; indeed, under existing conditions of scarcity and turnover of teachers, the training is designed not so much to train those who know to teach properly, as to show those who do not know how to teach what the system tells them. Furthermore, teacher training as given at present cannot be compared for interest and value with increased study of subjects or practical experience in the schools. Only if teacher training courses were a rewarding and challenging experience would the scholar find them useful. The fear that good scholars will not make good teachers is overdone. Indeed, it should never be forgotten that it is often those with no ability or knowledge to teach with who are most content to putter around with courses on methods.

The term "good scholar" should not, of course, be confined merely to the brilliant intellectual. The latter does not invariably make the best teacher; a better one may very well be the competent graduate with reasonably good, even if not first class, marks and with all round abilities admirably suited to teaching. What has to be warned against of course is the weak graduate who has barely scraped through his courses and who has passed in a little bit of everything but not much of anything. The safest method of selection is to aim for the able students and work down. To aim for the weak is to discourage the able; unfortunately an examination of the destination of the top and bottom graduates in almost any high school or university will amply illustrate that it is the lowest group which provides the most teachers. Thus does the state deprive itself of the possible services of an enormous group of able young people in the interest of and on the persistent advice of, people who are not teachers but administrators and who perpetuate their own dominance by carefully restricting the entrance to the system.

To illustrate, a brilliant young graduate in honour mathematics looks around for a possible career. Industry is interested in his subject and his record, and offers an attractive salary with regular increases. Suppose he also has a talent for teaching, for which he perhaps developed a liking by assisting a professor in tutoring and marking assignments. When he inquires about teaching jobs, he is told he must attend teachers' college and "learn how to teach." Some of his friends tell him teachers' courses are a waste of time and warn him that future advancement will depend more on "education" credits than on mathematical competence. Will he not almost invariably choose industry?

At the same time another young man is looking for a career. He has barely managed to scrape through his B.A. course—perhaps by repeating years and writing supplementals—and he has taken at most one or two courses in mathematics and passed them with third class or low honours standing. Industry does not beckon to a student with this record, and the doors of the graduate school are closed to him. But he can enter the "education" course with ease, and, after a liberal sprinkling of the history, philosophy, and psychology of education, accompanied by a quick résumé of school administration, and perhaps the writing of a thesis on something like "democracy in the algebra class," he can go into the school system as a "mathematics specialist." Such cases are so numerous as to render obvious yet another reason for the present crisis in the teaching of mathematics in the schools.

This situation also affects teachers with several years' experience who seek further training. They are encouraged, not to refresh themselves by renewed contact with the subjects they teach, but to take courses in "education." By and large, an M.Ed. will get a higher rating with the authorities than will an M.A. in a subject. A good teacher will not need the former, but he may need to have his mental horizons broadened in his field or to catch up with the changes which have occurred in it since he began to teach. Because of such a concentration on mechanics, many teachers are losing, as the years pass, the part of teaching ability which depends on the command of up-to-date knowledge, and replacing it with techniques which are little more than means of holding a place in a system.

Lack of sufficiently high standards and emphasis on quick, "practical" training are often excused because of the teacher shortage. The state, it is said, cannot insist on high standards because the number of available teachers would thereby be diminished. Comparison with other professions illustrates the fallacy of this argument and suggests that low standards may even be a cause of the shortage. In medicine and engineering, for example, where careful screening, high standards, and comparatively long training are involved, there is usually a surplus of students seeking admission. Theology illustrates the same point in another way: like "education," it is one of the easiest courses in university and it involves little screening and virtually no failures; there is also a perpetual shortage of students. The monetary rewards of a profession are only a partial explanation. A kind of educational equivalent of Gresham's Law dictates that weak courses and students drive out good courses and students; the state has yet found no way of amending it.

Statistics dramatically reveal that the system of training and licensing is not working. The simple fact is that, despite adjustments made to secure more teachers, nothing like the demand is being met either in quantity or in quality. Low prevailing standards notwithstanding, the United States was still short 20,000 secondary teachers and 45,000 elementary teachers when the schools opened in 1955.[14] A Canadian expert estimates that Canada will need an increase of 55,000 teachers within ten years.[15] Even where salaries have been raised substantially, as in Ontario, recruiting has been slow.[16] And, most serious of all, the high annual turnover of teachers, in Nova Scotia as much as 50 per cent in one year, makes recruiting and training practices as frustrating and inefficient as refilling a leaky vessel. It is obvious that demands for teachers cannot be met under present conditions; and that public authorities who on the one hand emphasize education for all children, the proliferation of courses, and the raising of the compulsory school age and, on the other hand, tolerate overcrowded classrooms, lowered standards, and staggered hours and double shifts because there are so few teachers, are being

[14]Educational Testing Service, *Annual Report*, 1954–5, p. 16.
[15]M. E. LaZerte, *Alberta Teachers' Association Magazine*, Jan., 1956, p. 14.
[16]Ottawa *Journal*, Dec. 29, 1959.

unreasonably optimistic. Whatever else it might be, the result for the pupils is not education.

The consequences of state control of teachers and their training join to depress the profession itself. Teacher trainees look for their future associations, not to a profession, but to a governmental hierarchy. Loyalty to a profession and a sense of membership in and dedication to it do not become sufficiently strong to hold the members, and they leave this profession in large numbers unheard of in any other. Without leadership from the profession there is little chance of the public's understanding the profession. The public will look to the state for leadership in education for the same reason the teachers do; it has all the power. Professional standards are, of course, just as important as leadership in forming public opinion; if teachers must accept the state's standards with their emphasis on techniques rather than learning, then the public will regard teachers accordingly.

The lack of professional spirit among teachers and the acceptance of governmental rather than professional standards thus set up a barrier against communication between teachers and the public. Important as teachers are to it, the community has not come to expect from them much leadership in their fields of knowledge. In many places the teacher is looked upon as a naïve amateur, rather than a competent authority, in what he teaches, and no amount of teaching ability can overcome this impression. Very few high school science teachers, for example, are consulted on technical matters by local industries. Equally seldom are English teachers invited to write for publications or history and civics teachers to do research for local authorities. As a result the community and the teachers lose the advantage which a combination of academic competence (where it exists) and practical application of knowledge could bring to both. Members of every other profession and trade, as well as most university teachers, make such contributions. Why cannot public school teachers do the same? It is only partly the fault of the teachers. "Teachers," said a distinguished educationist to the Canadian Teachers' Federation, "cannot expect prestige unless they deserve it and the tragic fact is that few of us deserve it. We have given up our interest in learning to concentrate on performing our routine tasks. And so we cannot compete with the learned men in our communities. . . . I am concerned with continuing intellectual interests. No person can be an effective teacher whose interests do not extend beyond the requirements of his textbook."[17] But the teachers are not free to develop these interests. Their routine is the way of life of the system and the textbook is its Bible.

The assumption by state officials of leadership in education has stunted the growth of the teaching profession just as perpetual babying by an over-zealous parent stunts the growth of a child's personality. Obedience to direction, acceptance of conformity, and reliance on political strategy in the school system take the place of the co-operation, example, professional efficiency, and *esprit de corps* found in bar associations, medical societies, and engineering institutes on the one hand, and the brotherhood and mutual strength of trade unions on the other.

This deplorable and illogical situation results in the teachers' federations being comparatively powerless, inconsequential organizations which the authorities can ignore at will and from which the public can expect little leadership. It is not their fault; they are doing all they can under conditions which permit them neither power nor prestige. Society therefore loses the valuable services which properly constituted and empowered teachers' organizations could give, and teaching suffers by being a leaderless, dependent, and dominated occupation.

[17]Marcus Long, "The Status of the Teaching Profession," *Educational Review* (N.B.) Sept.-Oct., 1955, p. 51.

6. The Twelve-Year Plan

STATE CONTROL OF SCHOOLS AND TEACHERS INEVITABLY INVOLVES state control of what is taught: the curriculum is, therefore, a government document, not a school's own programme. The purpose of the curriculum is ostensibly to furnish an official guide for schools and teachers indicating the requirements in each subject and each grade and thereby ensuring standardization of achievement throughout the system. This purpose seems inoffensive, even logical; but a short examination leads one to wonder to what extent it can really be achieved. One is led to ask, too, about how state control affects the curriculum and the teaching prescribed by it.

The first thing to be understood about the school curriculum is that there is no magic about it. It is simply an educational bill of fare similar to a restaurant menu. The description of the courses is, in both instances, merely a guide to what is *offered* and not an indication of what is obtained. In the restaurant the benefits to be gained depend on the skill of the cook, the ingredients used, and the tastes and appetites of the diners. Soup described as "chef's special" can be anything; "roast beef" may be the finest sirloin or cunningly disguised stewing meat. And every proprietor will testify that, whatever is provided, some customers are harder to please than others. In school, a course described as "British History" can be a vivid experience directed by a competent and stimulating historian or a dull, useless association with a textbook follower who knows nothing of the subject. Teachers, like cooks, are of all kinds; courses are combinations of many receipts; pupils possess every variety of taste, and may even suffer from academic dyspepsia.

It is difficult, however, for officials in a centrally controlled system to admit this variation which no amount of control can really prevent. They therefore tend to emphasize fixed common standards so that at least the illusion of sameness may be maintained. As a result, the school curriculum resembles a prescribed standard diet in which little or no distinction is made among institutions and those who teach and study in them. The effect is similar to what would result from offering the same menu at the Waldorf Astoria, Woolworth's soda fountains, and Daisy's Diner.

To ignore successfully the uncertainties of the curriculum in this fashion requires adroit salesmanship on the part of educational authorities. They exercise it by elevating and inflating the position of the curriculum out of all proportion to its significance. Like any other governmental programme it must be advertised and promoted. "Directors of curriculum" in every department of education specialize in it and curriculum committees multiply like rabbits. One professor of "education" goes so far as to admit,

The past two decades in the United States have witnessed almost feverish efforts at curriculum construction such as no period or place has ever seen before. . . . Many aims have been proposed, officially formulated, and published, often to the confusion of teachers, administrators, and the American people in general . . . more than fifteen hundred social objectives of English, more than three hundred aims of arithmetic in the first six grades, and more than eight hundred generalized aims of the social studies have been listed in courses of study. . . . On file in the curriculum bureau of an institution for the training of teachers are nearly fifty thousand curricula which have been prepared by committees and in most cases published and distributed during the past two decades. This interest in curriculum construction and reconstruction may be a healthy sign, but the general condition (which has not improved with the numerous writings and discussions on the curriculum) seems to reflect the absence of a consistent philosophy . . . from which the educational aims of this country derive.[1]

---

[1]E. W. Knight, *Twenty Centuries of Education* (Ginn, 1940), pp. 475-6.

It is surely not unreasonable to suggest that this immense effort is made necessary because the curriculum is constructed by too many people for too many people. Preoccupation with aims and programmes is a natural characteristic of large, centralized, organizations. Here once more Parkinson's law is clearly illustrated. The aims and programmes must justify the huge administrative machine and maintain the support of many people to whom the system must look well. Fine-sounding aims can be used to justify any policy, sustain any activity, or hide any defect, and there is nothing like what appears to be a well-organized programme to keep everybody together and busy. The politician comes to see in the curriculum something of the spell of the party platform; the departmental official finds that it provides unlimited scope for committees, surveys, and directives; the normal schools assist by providing endless courses on how to use it; many trustees regard an impressive curriculum as an indication of the respectability of their schools. The more elaborate it is the more admiring children and their parents are supposed to be and the more enthusiastic the taxpayers are expected to be with education itself. The theme of the curriculum could well be borrowed from Gilbert and Sullivan:

> Be happy all—the feast is spread before ye;
> Fear nothing, but enjoy yourselves, I pray!

It has to be admitted that it is, unfortunately, difficult for the state to avoid such treatment of the curriculum, and the reasons are by now familiar: political power over education means the dominance of political interpretations of the requirements of education; administration of a large system means emphasis on the mechanics and routine of operation.

The political interpretation, in so far as it affects the curriculum, is not difficult to assess. The politician's approach to young people is completely different from that of the teacher. Even though he may have children of his own, he soon develops in his public life the social service attitude, rose-coloured by a sense of power and good works, vote-directed by a desire for re-election, but at the same time shrewdly cautious under the influence of the demands of politics and people in the mass. The official's approach is an imitation of his superior's but, in addition, he is concerned with a system embracing all children and his approach to the requirements tends to be a constant search for an average. The politician wants something by way of a programme to please as many people as possible and he is all the happier if it can appear "democratic," practical, and not too difficult. The official wants it for ease of operation to be planned, set down, and authorized, and accompanied by the necessary instructions and guidebooks.

The convenient instruments for this kind of approach, and for its application on a wide scale, are the course and the textbook. At first sight they may appear necessary to ensure order, uniformity, and standards in the teaching done in many schools and by many teachers. On closer inspection, however, do they not reveal all the characteristics of prefabricated houses, cake mixes, and meccano sets? They simply involve teachers and pupils in putting together what someone else has prearranged. Teaching is thus confined to narrow limits and learning becomes a cut-and-dried routine. Most school work worthy of the name does not actually require such limitation and routine. Learning could be achieved more easily and quickly by wide and systematic reading of books, by constant practice in writing, and by frequent solving of problems, all directed by a teacher who knows what he is doing. The course should merely be a useful way of showing the category of such activity; to define all courses rigidly is to chop knowledge up into separate, and perhaps unrelated, sections. The textbook should be no more than a useful guide and summary; to emphasize it alone is to confine pupils to a narrow, monotonous programme and to one person's viewpoint. Nevertheless, curriculum planners seem to think that no subject can be covered unless it assumes the dignity and dimensions of a course complete with official text and with progress prescribed down to the exact pages. Thus the emphasis in learning is shifted to "taking" and "passing" courses, which inevitably become numerous, and may even become fashionable in order to attract attention. Educational officials come to prescribe them in much the same manner, and with much the same perspective, as the president of the Better Vision Institute who is quoted as saying that "the well-dressed young lady who wears glasses simply must have at least eight pairs to be correct"[2] or like the dean of a college of adult education who ran a school for church ushers in Halifax because they were the "forgotten men"[3] in many congregations.

The emphasis on "taking" things distorts standards. A pupil "takes" a subject, gets 50 per cent in the examinations and "passes," and, with the accumulation of sufficient "credits," he receives a certificate. This arrangement may be suitable for the convenient labelling of large numbers in a system. But its wisdom in education is surely doubtful because, under the circumstances, the work of teachers and pupils is too easily subordinated to the mere jumping of hurdles—which, because of the numbers who must clear them, cannot be placed too high. For the pupil, the minimum then tends to be the standard, and to "pass" means to get by at the 50 per cent level. As for the teacher, his work is judged too often on the number who jump the hurdles rather than on the height at which they jump.

The arithmetical accumulation of passes may be comforting to the authorities. Yet it is a meaningless standard because, impersonal as it must be, it cannot really indicate competence. A certificate holder may have learned a great deal working well under able teachers or virtually nothing plodding along under indifferent ones; indeed, he may even have done himself more harm than good by accumulating along the way wrong information and sloppy habits of thinking which his pass grades tend to conceal. The level at which courses are taught is certainly not indicated. It is easy to take and pass in many subjects and not go beyond the elementary stage in any one of them. Thus a pupil might follow an entire curriculum without learning the basic processes of education—how to learn and how to think.

In these facts there is surely an explanation of why so many young people are restless in school and complain of lack of challenge. They

[2]*Halifax Mail-Star*, Nov. 30, 1951.
[3]*Ottawa Journal*, Nov. 7, 1953.

know that the requirements of real life are entirely different from the requirements of the curriculum: in real life one "takes" in earnest or one is fired. The girl who gets 50 per cent in chemistry must, and knows she must, administer drugs with 100 per cent accuracy when she becomes a nurse; and the boy who "passes" in arithmetic must, and knows he must, make every calculation correctly when he gets a job in a bank. A brief from Calgary students to the recent Alberta Royal Commission on Education is typical of student opinion. Views of 365 students were asked. They welcomed more work and more discipline. Eighty per cent felt students not inclined to study should be dismissed from school. A majority suggested that entrance standards should be raised, that textbooks should be improved, and that courses should be confined to basic subjects with "frill courses" left to other agencies.[4] Pupils are not deceived by the slogan "learning can be fun"; they know that in all honesty it requires the same hard work, patience, and perseverance that they will need when wiring a house, winning a doubtful constituency, writing a book, or selling to an elusive customer in later life. Even the brightest pupils will not appreciate being able to coast along at the pace of the average; they know, or will soon find out, that the slow tortoises who work can always pass the able hares who sleep. Thus preparation for matriculation may be far from being the preparation for the "real life" of which the curriculum planners are so fond of talking; indeed under the circumstances matriculation is too often a threshold between make-believe and reality.

Strangely enough, however, "everyday life" is often used to justify the very conditions which are so remote from it. In official literature there is a constant shifting of emphasis away from the requirements of knowledge with their rigours and rewards and towards the "needs" and "aims" of the "common man" in "practical," "everyday life." Schooling thus becomes an adjustable process of distributing "useful" facts, notwithstanding that there are many interpretations of what is indeed useful and that no one has yet revealed anything more useful in education than the training of the

[4]*Ottawa Journal*, June 3, 1958.

mind itself. Consequently, many of the activities of the curriculum justified as "real-life situations" become a kind of artificial playing-at-games quite remote from the real challenge of life. These activities are easily overdone to the point where only the commonplace is regarded as knowledge and where the pupil becomes a slave to the familiar, suspicious, contemptuous, and afraid of the unfamiliar and difficult. C. S. Lewis describes the danger in his celebrated account of how devils tempt men. "They find it all but impossible," says one devil to another, "to believe in the unfamiliar while the familiar is before their eyes. Keep pressing home on him the *ordinariness* of things . . . don't let him get away from that invaluable 'real life' . . . give him a grand general idea that he knows it all and that everything he happens to have picked up in casual talk and reading is 'the results of modern investigation.' Do remember you are there to fuddle him."[5] The agents of darkness must have ample cause to be pleased with the dominance of this theme in pedagogical literature and in the curriculum itself.

The attempt to make learning agreeable and comfortable combines readily with the social-service outlook of the government to play down the abilities of pupils. Such misplaced benevolence appears on close inspection to be a tragic mistake, for it can limit capacity for education severely, and perhaps even destroy it.

Young people are older in outlook and more capable than adults think they are. Underestimating their abilities is a common mistake. But it is a special fault of educational officials, who, without the sympathy and practical outlook of the teacher and with a need for popular support, tend to be patronizing in attitude. Consequently, the prevailing policy in curriculum-making is to adjust courses and teaching methods to what officials think is the speed of the pupils, with little effort in the opposite direction: developing the speed of the pupils to the requirements of the work. "One of the aims of the school programme," explains a curriculum of the Ontario Department of Education, "is to provide for each individual those activities which are adapted to his particular capacities and in which he may

[5]C. S. Lewis, *The Screwtape Letters* (Fontana), p. 14.

participate with reasonable success and satisfaction." The weakness of this approach is indicated by one of its supporters who justifies it because "education must be founded upon pleasurable experiences, and upon activities in which pupils can achieve a reasonable measure of success."[6] Everyone knows of course that pupils should not be driven beyond the limits of their abilities into frustration. But "founding" education on pleasure and success in trivialities will get them nowhere and will produce frustration and boredom more readily than will challenging work. Artificial pleasure and "success" are not reliable developers of ability and character, and only impede maturity and postpone the day when pupils must take life seriously. Such a programme obscures the abilities of pupils and emphasizes what somebody else thinks they can do. The pupils' response is inevitable; they will rarely excel expectations without some challenge. "A pupil," wrote John Stuart Mill, "from whom nothing is ever demanded which he cannot do, never does all he can." Indeed the same is true of adults. "It holds good where anything is being done," explained Kipling, "if you give a man more than he can do, he will do it. If you only give him what he *can* do, he'll do nothing."

Again the curriculum differs from the requirements of real life. Pupils understand their operation in activities outside of school which they often find much more to their liking: here there are no politicians, officials, or psychologists to tell them what they cannot do and confuse them with artificial motivations. They know that ability in the high jump comes only with constant assault at heights beyond the initial capacity of the athlete, that it would be foolish to expect a change in the rules of hockey simply to suit the players, that there is something heroic about one who carries on after being kicked in the face or trampled in the mud on the football field, and that to deliver morning papers is to get up at five whatever the weather. They know too that whatever success they will have in later life, whether it be in surgery or in truck driving, largely depends on their adjusting their abilities to the job. They also know

[6]H. L. Stein, "Educational Psychology," in Katz (ed.), *Canadian Education Today* (Toronto: McGraw-Hill, 1956), p. 48.

that the same should really be true of school work; they should adjust themselves to the demands of mathematics or carpentry if they are to gain anything from them. But here the standards asked by their elders are artificial; these courses are watered down to suit supposed abilities or to give all students delusions of happiness though some are incompetent; all they need to strive for is, not perfection, but that mark of mediocrity, the "pass." The curriculum therefore does not do what it professes; rather than promote the growth of underdeveloped abilities it caters to them.

Policy makers and curriculum planners are, then, more benevolent than realistic in imposing their ideas of children's capacity on the schools. One suspects, again, that the artificial demands of the large system have blinded them to the natural requirements of education. Nature will not slow down to the pace set by the departments of education. Indeed she sets her own arbitrary deadline for most subjects; if pupils meet it they can learn the subject; if they do not they cannot. Under such circumstances official benevolence is really making schooling *harder*, not easier. This deadline can be illustrated physically by a crossed eye. An oculist can straighten a crossed eye of a child up to eight years of age and the child's brain can soon develop the sight of that eye from its previous low almost to normal. After the age of eight, however, the eye can be straightened for the sake of appearance, but the sight in it can never be restored.

We now know that this same kind of deadline exists in the learning of languages, and, because it is not being met in the schools, we are forced to the conclusion that most of the curriculum requirements in language are serving little more than appearance. The neurologists, of whom Dr. Wilder Penfield can be referred to especially, tell us that the parts of the brain concerned with communication are most efficient before the age of from twelve to fourteen; afterwards those parts harden and function with increasing difficulty. Children who learn to speak their own language from two to four years of age can certainly learn others before they are fourteen, provided, of course, that they are taught by persons who are really fluent in the languages. Children learn to speak languages incredibly quickly; with any encouragement a child of six could pick up even conversational Chinese or Greek in a year. Put two children of different languages in a playroom together and each will learn a small vocabulary in a few hours and almost without effort. In school, however, young people are only starting languages at thirteen, and must spend the next few years labouring over the elementary declensions and conjugations which they could have picked up more naturally with more ease and interest a few years earlier. And they are taught in most cases by teachers who themselves know little of the language concerned. Thus a high school student taking elementary French is learning nothing more than a two-year-old French child and there is little possibility of his learning it as well! Language therefore becomes, not an instrument of communication and a training of lifetime value, but a boring, unrewarding routine to be dropped as soon as possible.

Is this failure to meet a natural deadline not a probable reason for obvious difficulties in other subjects? There is considerable evidence, for instance, that the long, playful approach to arithmetic and then to mathematics has put North American children from three to five years behind where they should be in those subjects. Anyone can find the answer to the question by starting piano lessons at eighteen and seeing how hard it is to get the mind, ears, and fingers adjusted to the techniques ten years too late. The principle that "you can't teach an old dog new tricks" is important in education, and it should be applied from grade one. Neglect of this principle has often been criticized of course, usually on the ground that learning is made too easy, too comfortable and ineffective. But cannot the prevailing policy of benevolence be more logically criticized on the ground that by ignoring the deadlines, it makes learning actually more difficult in many subjects and almost impossible in some? The easy approach has proved in practice to be the hard approach because the pupils are too old to respond satisfactorily to the instructions they receive.

The fruit of the policy is most evident, as might be expected, in the end results. At junior matriculation a fifth or more of the candidates generally fail, and approximately two-thirds of those who pass attain third class standing which, after twelve long years of schooling, is scarcely a satisfactory level at which to enter upon the responsibilities of life. Such results are not surprising because, in the years when children look for or dream about challenge and adventure, they have been taught by means of a highly artificial method of cultivation in hot-house conditions and their process of learning has been an unnatural adherence to rigid official requirements. The prevailing force in their schooling is nurture rather than nature, and the product resembles what Disraeli called "the monotony of organized platitude."

Consider, for example, prescribed readers used in language. The six-year-old, who already knows a good story when he hears one, encounters a "curriculum foundation series" of which the following is a fair sample:

> Come, Puff.
> Come and go up.
> Go up, up, up.
> Come down, down, down.
> Go up and down.

Such anaemic experiences of Puff and his pals Spot, Dick, and Jane occupy many months because a little pedagogical dance must be performed around every precious morsel of information. They are scarcely a worthy introduction to either language or literature: they are full of baby talk, they encourage bad reading habits which will have to be broken later, and they give the child a poor impression of the kind of literature he may expect to encounter in school. Triviality and lack of thought and imagination are also features of the "guidebooks" which teachers must use to teach from such readers. In one of them a page of artful prompting is necessary to show the teacher how to explain the "learning situation" caused by a cat in a tree, on the apparent assumption that the teachers and children can never grasp anything for themselves. I have frequently criticized these readers when speaking at teachers' conventions and Home and School meetings. Invariably the grade one teachers have come to me afterwards expressing their agreement with me. Invariably, too, any school superintendent or departmental official who happens to be present stoutly defends the readers and the methods required to teach them.

During the years which follow this introduction, the learning of language becomes a slow and carefully measured progress through a series of readers which are far too immature for the pupils, and accompanying workbooks which keep everybody in lockstep—so many words a lesson, so many spellings a week, regardless of the abilities of the teachers and pupils. The average twelve-year-old, for instance, has probably read many of the "Hardy Boys" series, and he is certainly capable of reading *Swiss Family Robinson, Kon-Tiki, Ascent of Everest,* and the like. Instead he must be content in school with a sampling of pathetic little stories, while the books he is ready for are postponed until high school at which time it is really too late to develop the habit of reading extensively. He has been using the telephone for six years or more but only in grade seven is he told the following:

> In the modern world the telephone plays a very important part. Hardly a day goes by without our finding it necessary to make social or business calls. We telephone friends. We telephone the butcher or the grocer. We telephone the dentist. If this most useful of modern inventions were removed, how lost we should feel.

At that stage he may even be calling a girl to make a date for the movies while his family waits impatiently for him to hang up. Evidently, however, the textbook writer and the director of curriculum have no children, for the pupil is asked in school to "choose a partner and prepare to dramatize one of the telephone conversations listed below." This exercise, called a "language journey," is a belated experience which would have been more interesting and fruitful in grade two. A little later, at the age of fifteen, language could be a fascinating programme of reading, including full biographies of great explorers and statesmen and books about such institutions as Scotland Yard and Florence Nightingale's nursing profession. Instead there are texts and anthologies containing bits and pieces in "digest" form. As a result, the pupil is sampling and not enjoying a full story, being guided cautiously into things and never plunging into them himself, and being confronted with the arranged and the expected at a time when the unplanned surprise moves him more. At last, when matriculation is reached at the age of eighteen, the pupil studies to be examined on some required tidbits from a very narrow range of literature when, with any amount of encouragement, he could be reading and understanding books at a rate of at least one a week. Thus have innumerable pupils struggled through a maze of techniques starting with the uncertainties of "reading readiness" and ending with the frustrations of "remedial English." Small wonder, therefore, that reading is so difficult to so many that the digest, the picture magazine, and the comic book form the standard literary fare in the age of "universal education."

The dilatory approach is accompanied by what might be called the "water-wings theory" of education which assumes that nothing can be learned without aids, motivations, and projects. But learning is largely a matter of receiving certain information and letting nature take its course. The teacher who, with guidebook in hand, parades every little shred of knowledge, turns every trivial experience into a "learning situation," and carefully administers every word and lesson in the precise prescriptions of a rigid curriculum leaves little for the mind of the pupil to do by itself. Aids to learning, like water-wings to swimmers, have their limited uses, but those who must rely on them are helpless without them and cannot venture far.

Indeed, aids to learning have characteristics recently noted by medical men in tranquillizing drugs. The latter, we are now told, are effective when used in moderate amounts for specific purposes and when followed by adequate treatment. But they are dangerous when patients become over-dependent on them or suffer a reaction to them which is worse than the original ailment, or when they weaken a patient's morale and emotions. They can also undermine the professional ethics of the physician who is under pressure to prescribe them and who gets into the habit of using them without justification. They may even encourage society to avoid anxiety and challenge by self-delusion rather than by facing realities. The analogy can easily be traced in the field of pedagogy.

Aids to learning are usually defended on the assumption that they are needed to rouse and maintain the interest of the pupils. In moderation they do perform this function. But in excess the interest artificially stimulated tends itself to be artificial. It is also temporary. The aids soon become boring because too little is left to challenge the effort and imagination of the individual. Drawing is an example. Colouring books are useful for a time. But they create neither a permanent interest nor a skill because someone else has done the real drawings and all the children do is fill them in by colouring them. One child's reaction seems both inevitable and typical: "Do you like painting?" asked Sir William Orpen of a little girl watching him at work. "No," was the frank reply, "we have to do it in school."

A further recommendation often put forward on behalf of detailed directions and "helpful" aids is their necessity for uneducated and untrained teachers. This is a poor, indeed terrible, excuse which only points up the weakness of the system as a whole. A curriculum will no more make up for a poor teacher than will a good programme for a poor concert singer.

The effect of the lag of curriculum requirements behind the abilities of children goes beyond the learning of individual subjects; it extends to the general level of maturity permitted in a whole generation. When, we should ask, is a young person ready for adult life? What age is the most productive in the human being? Does schooling enable young people to start life early enough, or does it prolong childhood unduly by erecting obstacles to maturity? There was a time when it was common for young people to finish school at fourteen with just as much, and in many cases more, knowledge than they have now, and be well advanced in their business or military careers by eighteen. It was common to graduate from college in the teens and be married by twenty. Many "made their mark" long before they were thirty; numerous inventors, explorers, poets, painters, and musicians were very young men when they achieved greatness. It was possible for William Pitt to become Prime Minister at twenty-four, Mr. Mackenzie King to be a Deputy Minister at twenty-six, John D. Rockefeller to start work at sixteen and be president of his own company at twenty-six. The winners of responsible government, the fathers of Confederation, and the founding fathers of the United States were almost all young men. Indeed, Sir William Osler, a shrewd judge of people as well as a great doctor, has said that all the main advances of the world came from men under forty and a large proportion of the world's evils from men over sixty.

Today, however, we have a different outlook on age. It is almost impossible for a young person to embark on a trade before he is eighteen or on a professional career before he is twenty-five. High school graduates are normally eighteen; all their courses notwithstanding, they still have to learn a trade or start near the bottom in business; four years of college takes them to twenty-two; the professions require another four years of study at least, and postgraduate work may take another year or two. Thirty or thereabouts becomes the marriage age for many professional men (unless they marry as students) and they are almost middle-aged when their children are growing up; their youth is passed before they start their life's work; and they have only thirty-five years ahead of them before the age of retirement.

There is something wrong somewhere. Schooling is pushing the childhood years into the teens and every other stage ahead a decade. This delay is not caused so much by the extra training required in many professions and occupations, but rather by the inflation of primary work in the schools. The lack of progress beyond the elementary stage in all subjects puts an added burden on employers and colleges who cannot assume that matriculants have an adequate background. It appears, too, that this delay is one of the reasons why narrow specialization is permitted at the expense of liberal education. The student has to specialize in his later years of study so as to learn enough of something to get a job; it is too late for him to start a liberal education in college and professional school; grade five is the place to begin.

Nature's programme is different from that of the schools. Girls mature from twelve up and boys from fourteen up. Dating starts at this stage and "going steady" is clear evidence of growing up. Anyone who has done business with an alert teenager of eighteen who has had any experience finds that he is well able to use all his faculties and a large measure of common sense. He has not the judgment of some adults; but he has more judgment than other adults, and he is as keen and alert as he will ever be and quite able to hold his own with many of his elders. The body and brain are at their best at eighteen, the senses are keen, the judgment and reflexes are quick, and initiative and enthusiasm are at their peak.

The knowledge and experience acquired at school are, however, far behind physical development. According to our social and educational system young people are only high school pupils. They are still being taught everything, all their activities are still regulated, and they have as yet been given little responsibility and experience of their own. Although they have been in school for almost a dozen years, they are still at only the elementary stage in all their subjects and are involved in much routine at a time when they are ready for the more advanced stage of using their judgment.

The attitude of young people to the routine shows how unpromising is the emphasis placed upon it. Stephen Leacock caught the general effect:

How strange it is, our little procession of life. The child says, "When I am a big boy". But what is that? The big boy says "When I grow up". And then, grown up, he says, "When I get married". But to be married, what is that after all? The thought changes to "When I'm able to retire". And then, when retirement comes, he looks back over the landscape traversed; a cold wind seems to sweep over it; somehow he has missed it all, and it is gone. Life, we learn too late, is in the living, in the tissue of every day and hour. So it should be with education.

But so it is not; a false view discolours it all. For the vastly greater part of it the students' one aim is to get done with it. There comes a glad time in his life when he has "finished" mathematics, a happy day when he has done philosophy, an exhilarating hour when he realizes that he is finished with "compulsory English". Then at last his four years are out, his sentence expired, and he steps out of college a free man without a stain on his character—and not much on his mind. Later on, he looks back wistfully and realizes how different it might have been.

What, it should be asked, about those who *have* got the most out of education and out of life? One suspects that very few of them had to exclaim "When I am a big boy"; it is altogether likely that right at the start they were using their faculties and experiencing life to the maximum extent that their age permitted.

The purposes of education cannot be achieved by setting this lethargic pace. Nor can the pace be justified by reason of a system to be maintained, an average to be catered to, or a political responsibility to be met. The maximum quality and quantity of education obtainable by each child according to his ability and his effort should override in importance any considerations of governmental social service. Again we are led to the familiar conclusion that political considerations are being permitted to displace educational ones. In other words, social service in education is too much social and not enough service.

Control by the state of what is taught has shifted attention from the teacher to the curriculum with substantial effect on both class-room teaching and professional morale. Pupils of a much earlier age were attracted to a scholar with the idea that they would study under him, or apprenticed themselves to a skilled artisan from whom they could secure adequate training. The teacher then was a master, leader, and guide; he was held in awe by his disciples who looked to him for knowledge; he was respected by the community which placed him among its prominent citizens. Today, however, pupils go to school to follow the state's programme and fulfil the state's requirements. The teacher now is not expected to be a master of knowledge: he might rather be described as a master of ceremonies prompted by official script writers.

Important elements of good teaching such as initiative, imagination, and deep personal interest in both the subjects and the pupils are easily lost to use under this arrangement. The shackling of good teachers to the routine plan, if it does not confine their abilities, forces them to find ways of getting round the requirements; fortunately for their pupils, many of them, with the help of discerning principals, are able to do just this. But their talents are too valuable to run the risk of being misused, like those of a good pianist forced to sit at a player piano pushing the pedals while the music comes from a roll of paper in which someone else has made the appropriate holes.

It is widely assumed that teachers have a major part in planning the school curriculum. In fact they do not. Practically all published studies on curricula come from professional "educators." All the final requirements come from officials. Teachers are sometimes consulted by means of questionnaires or curriculum committees. But there is little they can do on their own. They can only recommend; they have no power to adopt. Indeed, there is much evidence that if teachers had authority over their own curricula there would be many changes. It is reported, for instance, that more than half the teachers questioned in a recent survey did not approve of the courses of study in history organized in the Canadian provinces.[7] Pupils evidently agree with the teachers, for Canadian history is not a popular subject in the public schools.

Featuring the curriculum instead of the teachers has gone as far as offering courses without teachers to teach them. It should be obvious that the value of any course is no higher than that of the teaching. A course in "the history of civilization designed to awaken the interest of the young citizen in his democratic heritage" is just so much waste time if it is taught by someone who does not know what she is talking about. It is folly for a school board to offer a course in carpentry if it cannot secure a skilled man to give it. Yet it is a national phenomenon that the curriculum has become more and more elaborate as the shortage of teachers grows.

There is no escaping the fact that the curriculum has to be designed at the present time in the face of two conflicting circumstances: the shortage of teachers and the greatly increased number of pupils. Nevertheless, as earlier pages have indicated, the state is not in a position to try to resolve this conflict; politics won't permit it. Curriculum planners are therefore forced to ignore obvious weaknesses wherever they occur and keep up appearances. A department or school board will not, indeed cannot, announce that French will

[7]M. Katz, *The Teaching of Canadian History in Canada* (Winnipeg: University of Manitoba Press, 1953), p. 10.

not be given this year because Miss Lafleur died and a suitable replacement cannot be secured. Instead it will assign the course to whatever teacher is available regardless of her knowledge of French. Nor can the authorities, who must make room for increased numbers, admit a higher failure rate, or frankly state that the quality of the courses offered depends on the quality of the pupils and the work they do. That would be "undemocratic." But, no matter what the curriculum may indicate, a course in grade nine arithmetic taught to thirty pupils competent in grade eight arithmetic is entirely different from one given to fifteen who know their grade eight work and fifteen who do not. Yet automatic grading, which creates the latter situation, prevails everywhere and pupils who have failed or just barely passed are allowed to carry on. An accumulation of credits thus displaces the teachers and the standards as the theme of the curriculum, and the state is not able to do much about it.

The final expression of state control of the curriculum and the ultimate blow to good standards, good teaching, and effective learning is the elaborate system of departmental examinations. The present school system automatically requires such examinations. The state cannot say that Johnny Brown studied English successfully for four years with Miss Sarah Smith, the celebrated English teacher at Central High, and therefore should know the subject. Nor can Miss Smith teach Johnny in such a way as to give him the maximum possible training which four years will permit. That would, of course, be learning and teaching at their best. The system cannot notice Johnny or Miss Smith; it can only certify if the boy jumps an arbitrary hurdle called an examination. The boy is not, therefore, a student of the teacher's; he is a candidate for the examination, which is a very different thing. The teacher, in turn, is not teaching for competence, but for passing. Inevitably, therefore, the examinations govern the teaching instead of the teaching determining the examinations. The objectionable element, it must be emphasized, is not the fact that there are examinations, which are unavoidable, but that they are based on arbitrary, mechanical, official requirements rather than on teaching.

Teaching for examinations defeats the whole purpose of education. It encourages a standardization because the examiners must be concerned with a province-wide or state-wide average and it ultimately produces a dead level of mediocrity because every student is forced to study the same required bits of information in the same way. Good teachers cannot afford to teach the subjects in the way they think will ensure competence since a pass in general examinations is gained, not by competence, but by the mechanical production of required facts about limited topics. Poor teachers may therefore teach from old examination papers and, by careful drill in prepared questions, which will be effective only until the examinations are over, get enough pupils "through" to satisfy their boards. A teacher, who is unprotected from official and parental pressure, will be judged by the pass rate of his pupils rather than their knowledge, and will find the examinations a convenient excuse for avoiding the responsibility of using his own judgment in promoting or failing pupils. The examination hall becomes the judgment seat, the question becomes the standard of learning, and the pass mark of 50 per cent becomes the great goal. The examinations, however, are unworthy of all this honour. They test only the temporary knowledge of the moment; they are based on a limited range of facts; they cannot allow for differences in schools and teachers; and they are usually administered, set, and marked, not to test what the student knows about a subject, but merely what he knows about what a curriculum office requires. Unfortunately, too, it is easy to manipulate examinations. If something goes wrong with the results, scaling is a common remedy for increasing the pass rate. If poor teaching and inadequate study result in a low passing rate, any official or parent can raise a general complaint that examinations are too hard and secure a lessening of the requirements. There were province-wide complaints in Ontario and Nova Scotia in 1956. Weaknesses are inevitable in tests of any kind, but they are aggravated in the case of these all-important examinations by the prevailing emphasis on the curriculum which causes the mechanics of examinations to overshadow both the quality and working conditions of teachers and the effort of which pupils are capable. The shortage of mathematics teachers, for instance, is now desperate. Inevitably, therefore, the quality of instruction in this subject has diminished sharply. Yet in three provinces, the annual reports of the Atlantic Provinces Examining Board indicate that the marks in matriculation algebra and geometry improved steadily in the past ten years. Thus these marks show how requirements have been met while the far more important factor of how mathematics has been taught has been obscured.

Let us consider matriculation history as an illustration of the general routine. The official requirements do not specify that Mary Jones must be taught by a teacher who knows history, that she should read widely in a given period, that she should understand certain basic concepts which explain most historical events, and that at the end of grade twelve she should have a fairly general workable knowledge of the subject. This arrangement could be guaranteed by any competent teacher and any reasonably conscientious pupil *if they were left alone.* But no such happy partnership is possible. The requirements specify that Mary will be "responsible for" certain allotted pages of an authorized text under the supervision of whatever teacher the school board hires and assigns. The teacher, especially if she knows little history, will pick her careful way through every line and page, adhering to the opinions and descriptions of the author, telling the pupils to underline "the important things," and drilling the questions which are likely to be asked on the examinations. Mary spends a whole year, sometimes more, with the one author and the one teacher's interpretation of that one author, reading the required pages over and over again, memorizing lists of kings and prime ministers without becoming acquainted with any of them, learning the particulars of wars without really knowing how they started or what both sides were fighting for, marshalling facts about social or political events such as the signing of Magna Carta and the achieving of responsible government without understanding their significance, and all the time noting details, not because they are interesting and valuable information, but because they "might be asked." Small wonder that the chances are that Mary will never look at another history book as long as she lives.

Meanwhile a department or an examining board has asked a

"setter" to arrange a paper in history based on the assigned pages of the assigned book. He can do little more than disguise the same questions which were asked on the same subject in former years. He dares not be too original because he might confuse the pupils (now called "candidates") who have not been prepared for the unexpected; he must be careful about testing ingenuity lest he be accused of asking "trick questions"; and he must phrase his questions so that they obviously bear on the course, are easy to answer and easy to mark. He knows, too, that his paper will be passed around a government office, that it will be published after the examinations, and that it will be studied and memorized in hundreds of classrooms the following year.

When Mary has "written" history, her paper is bound in huge bundles of similar papers and sent to a central marking depot. Here, in midsummer, a group of "markers" assemble and read thousands of papers all saying the same things about the same things. For weeks on end they give so many marks for this and take off so many marks for that. Ultimately Mary's paper comes to the top of the pile. She is just one more unknown candidate, the product of an unknown school, the pupil of an unknown teacher. Has she answered the required number of questions in the required way? Are the familiar facts already encountered a thousand times on her paper? The red pencil hovers over each page, thirteen marks out of twenty for this question, six out of ten for that one, and the whole adds up to 58 per cent. And so on to the next paper, and the next, and the next until they are all marked. The results are entered on appropriate forms and tallied. Post-mortems are held by the markers: Have enough candidates passed? If not, was it a fair paper? Did it follow the curriculum faithfully? Do the results need to be adjusted? What will the department think? the teachers? the parents? the pupils? the public? The simple question "does Mary Jones know any history?" is buried in this huge mechanical operation, for she is only a statistic. Even she will likely have long ceased worrying about what history did for her, and will be content with the appearance of her name on a pass list, the coveted but modest reward for all the effort involved, the anti-climax to twelve years with the curriculum.

The characteristics of the curriculum as we know it raise the question of the motive behind it. Presumably it is the educating of children. But, as with all good works, is there not a danger of another motive overshadowing the professed one—a political motive involving the urge to control? To state the question bluntly, are departments of education and offices of school superintendents devoting their energies to the actual function of educating or are they, unwittingly perhaps, succumbing to an old instinct of officialdom and building an elaborate machinery to manipulate a lot of people? Governments must cater to and organize the masses to a certain extent if any degree of order is to prevail, but this surely does not apply in the present instance. To use the curriculum as an instrument of control is to serve neither the state nor the masses because children are started in life with a wrong approach to their responsibilities as citizens. The masses are ill served when control is emphasized to the point where it discourages individualism and freedom and emphasizes an average without doing enough to raise that average. The children of the masses are ill served when the degree and kind of control undermine respect for their intellectual capacity by minimizing the number who are capable of real study and emphasizing the dependence of all pupils on the state. Under such circumstances is it to be wondered at that the natural resistance to state-controlled education mentioned earlier should contribute to a substantial drop-out of pupils from the upper grades?

The element in the curriculum which does most to encourage control and undermine intellectual capacity is uniformity. State education insists upon it and instils it in children. Taxpayers are too readily persuaded that it is necessary if the system is to be "efficient" and "democratic." Uniformity is not efficient because it confines ability; it is not democratic for it restricts freedom; it is not equality of opportunity, but the negation of it, for it limits men. Uniformity soon becomes conformity, and its victims become obsessed with the idea that there must be something wrong if they are not like others and not doing what everyone else does. Much emphasis is placed on getting children "socially adjusted" and seeing that they conform to a norm. People are anything but well-adjusted these days, however, a fact supported by the boom in psychiatry and the public expenditure in North America of $125 million in a year on tranquillizers.

"Social adjustment" makes its *début* with great fanfare in the curriculum, and uniformity in the schools keeps it constantly before the children. Unfortunately, it often stands in the way of wisdom and common sense and prevents people from securing happiness in getting along with themselves as well as with others and from finding satisfaction in making the most of their own abilities. People spend the larger portion of their lives communicating with themselves, and no amount of "social adjustment" will help the person who cannot live with himself. Citizenship is not a fuzzy kind of *camaraderie* to be valued according to how prominent or popular one becomes, but a participation in society which results from the maximum use of one's powers and opportunities. Maladjusted individuals will never make a well-adjusted group, but neither will over-adjusted individuals. Nor will either make a strong group; it is tragically easy to manipulate a group to the point where it becomes a mere herd—unthinking, easily managed, and readily stampeded. At this point democracy dies. "The greatly-gifted," wrote Lionel Barrymore after a long life and unique opportunities for studying men, "are not the fortunate persons of this world. Today we are forced to read all these astute papers in the magazines about the values of 'adjustment'. We must all, it seems, 'adjust' ourselves to the world and to everybody else. How fortunate, I say, for the sheep who can munch in unison and adjust. How painful for the artists, the statesmen, the pioneers, the musicians, and the actors who fail to keep time—but what a gift for us that they do fail."[8]

The state curriculum is now perfectly designed for munching in unison. It is unrivalled as an instrument for manipulating people; it regiments children from the outset of their lives and emphasizes control rather than education. That it should be tolerated in the name of "democratic education" is surely one of the most ironic paradoxes of our time.

[8]Lionel Barrymore, *We Barrymores* (New York: Appleton-Century, 1951), p. 282.

7. Control

Without

Dominance

THE QUESTION "WHAT CAN BE DONE ABOUT IT?" WILL SURELY HAVE
presented itself at many points in this book. It is time now for us to
consider a possible solution for the problems described. I do have a
proposal to present and in presenting it, I confine its description to an
outline of the general principles and characteristic administrative
structure involved. The details can be worked out later, of course, by
those who would put the proposal into effect and according to
conditions in local areas.

The plan is based on the approved approach to a well-known
problem of government: the difficulty for those who govern to
know when to do things themselves and when and how to trust
others. Too much government concentrates power and the hands
which hold it are not invariably capable; too little invites chaos.
Students of democracy have long urged the division of power so as
to minimize the danger of abuse of it and to strengthen it through
the capabilities and influence of diverse talents and opinions. "If
government," wrote Alexander Hamilton, "is in the hands of the
few, they will tyrannise over the many; if in the hands of the many,
they will tyrannise over the few. It ought to be in the hands of both,
and they should be separated."

In no area of the operation of government is this observation more important than in education. Power over the minds, talents, and opinions of people is far more significant than power over their purses, their commerce, or their bodies. That power, therefore, should be respected and properly located if tyranny of either the few or the many is not to destroy democracy by first destroying education. Previous chapters have given a description of how the schools we know today lie powerless between a tyranny of the few in the form of an official dominance unique in government and a tyranny of the many represented by a limitless scope for public pressure perhaps unmatched in any other social activity. Is it not possible to find a way to preserve in education the same provisions for the wise and effective use of power which have been found indispensable elsewhere in government?

Educational reform would seem to require two types of change. The one most frequently suggested involves methods of instruction and conditions of teaching with emphasis on the schools and their staffs. The other is equally important but is far less obvious to the general public: a change in the administration of education away from emphasis on the government and its agencies. It is also not noted enough that the first change is virtually impossible without the second because the kind of schooling children are to get depends now as much on the policies and actions of officials as on the work of teachers. In suggesting improvements in public education, therefore, we must surely deal first with government and second with schools.

The state's participation in education is not, of course, a unique venture in non-political matters. As has been indicated earlier, governments have long been involved in economic life, especially in transportation, electric power, certain industrial developments, and the like which cannot be left exclusively in private hands; because they involve public policy and also great risk, enormous expenditure, and limited profits in providing services needed by the whole populace, control by the people is imperative. This type of activity provoked much controversy in its earlier stages and there is still discussion about the relative merits of private enterprise and governmental control in certain activities. It has always been recognized that politics and business do not invariably mix to the advantage of both, and it has come to be accepted that when they do mix, provision must be made to ensure the advantages of both by a combination of public ownership and responsibility with the practical benefits of business interest and initiative.

Direct control by parliament and administration through departments, the traditional instruments of governmental action, had to be modified, it was found, when the state entered into business. They related to the political life as exercised in government, and their characteristics were not entirely suited to the life of practical economics. Members of legislatures had neither the time nor the knowledge to delve into the intricacies of business, and their dependence on votes did not always permit them to take required steps in operations really non-political in kind. Civil servants were not business men either, and they were not free enough from political direction and the routines of their offices to exercise the initiative necessary for full efficiency in commerce. Although the state still had final responsibility, it came to be recognized that its institutions had been established for definite functions and that new functions required new institutions.

Among these new institutions was the public trust, a body owned but not directly managed by the government, which was designed to combine government and business so as to guarantee responsibility to the public and economic efficiency. The Central Electricity Board in England, the Canadian National Railways, and the Tennessee Valley Authority in the United States were early and important public trusts which not only managed great enterprises, but also served as experiments in public business and as models after which other bodies were fashioned. The principles on which they operated were also applied when the government as owner took on activities other than business, such as medicine (public hospitals), culture and entertainment (the broadcasting corporations), and even education (the public universities). Thousands of such institutions have been established since the First World War, and they are now accepted for better or for worse as essential instruments of public enterprise.

The organization of public trusts varies widely. Broadly speaking, however, each of them is constituted by statute as a government-owned body corporate managed by a board of trustees, governors, or directors with specified powers and direct responsibility for conducting the business concerned, and with an administrative organization of its own. Provision is made for responsibility to a legislature, always through public audit and annual report, and also, in some cases, by dependence on the House for financial appropriation. The members of the board are sometimes experts in the activities involved; more often they are public-spirited laymen selected because of their ability or experience or because they represent certain interest groups. The board appoints a president or manager and such other officers and staff as might be necessary, and all personnel are responsible to the board through their chief executive. Politicians and civil servants usually have no direct control over the activities of such organizations; indeed, some statutes expressly forbid them to sit on the board. The board's moneys and accounts are kept separate from those of the government so that they can be handled according to the needs of the activity rather than those of the departments of government.

This type of organization is designed on the principle that, if government must become involved in a certain activity outside its normal terms of reference, it should be prepared, in the interest of both the service and the public for whom it is performed, to delegate its authority to a body which can act independently of political pressure and departmental routine, and yet not as a private monopoly. Such a board is in a better position than government to deal with other non-governmental organizations; it will be more familiar with the technical requirements for operation; it can ensure a sustained interest in the field concerned, with ensuing benefits in performance; it must keep abreast of public opinion and yet it can also influence it; it can deal with emergencies immediately without having to wait for the slow operation of official sanction; it can avoid the rigidity which often results from continuous and detailed

scrutiny for political purposes and many of the dangers of interference by selfish pressure groups working through politics. The
distinguished British authority on public administration, W. A.
Robson, has written:

> The complex technological problems involved, the need for a spirit of boldness
> and enterprise, the desire to escape from the excessive caution and circumspection
> which day-to-day responsibility to Parliament necessitates, the recognition that
> the operation of public utilities and industrial undertakings requires a more flexible
> type of organization than that provided by the ordinary Whitehall department—
> these were the principal causes which led to the establishment of the independent
> public service board and helped to gain public favour. On the whole, the political
> instinct which led to the setting up of these boards has been amply justified by the
> results which have been achieved.[1]

There is a possible risk, of course, in the removal of such an
enterprise too far from legislative control. Actually the ever present,
though infrequently exercised, right of the legislature to ask questions, appropriate funds, and alter the statute concerned minimizes
that risk and ensures an outlet for the ventilation of serious grievances,
an opportunity to remedy mistakes, and a stimulus to responsible
administration. The risk of politically minded interference, however,
has always been adjudged greater than that of irresponsibility.
"Insofar as fears were expressed about the central question of
control," wrote one observer of the establishment of the British
Broadcasting Corporation in 1926,[2] "these almost all took the form,
not that the Corporation would be too irresponsible, but that it
would be too subservient to the will of the Minister or the Government." The minister through whom the Corporation was to be
responsible to parliament himself urged that the Corporation be
granted "the maximum of freedom" and "the greatest possible
latitude in regard to the conduct of their own affairs." Sir Robert
Borden expressed the same policy prior to the passing of the Canadian National Railways Act in 1919:

> We do not intend to operate the . . . System directly under a department of the
> Government. . . . There will be a reconstituted board of directors. We shall
> endeavour to get the best men we can and we shall not interfere with them. We

[1] W. A. Robson, *Public Enterprise* (London: George Allen and Unwin, 1937), p. 363.
[2] Terence O'Brien, *British Experiments in Public Ownership and Control* (London: George
Allen and Unwin, 1937), pp. 108–9.

shall leave the administration and operation of that road to be carried on absolutely under the Board of Directors and we shall use every means available to the Government . . . in order that anything like political influence, political patronage, or political interference . . . shall be absolutely eliminated.[3]

When government first entered the field of culture, it encountered conditions even more foreign to its traditional functions than were the activities of business. Presenting a radio programme was very different from constructing a highway, and developing an art was in no way similar to encouraging an industry. Politics was usually concerned with tangible and practical projects which could be evaluated, planned, and carried out. Culture, on the other hand, involved intangibles affecting the artistic talents, the tastes and the emotions of individuals and groups and these have always been difficult to measure and direct, let alone satisfy. It was obvious that government would be particularly ineffective in this field. When the British government first became involved with broadcasting, for instance, it was realized that an agency associated with the communication of ideas is concerned "not with a single social need and sphere of action, but with the whole range of intellectual interests of the individuals associated together in the community which it serves."[4] Such a function would be incomprehensible to a government department, and broadcasting was finally placed under the same type of independent management as publicly owned business enterprises.

When government assumed responsibility for university education it followed a similar procedure. Legislatures established and empowered the public universities and provided funds by annual appropriation. Much success followed when governments left them alone, departments of education had no significant control over them, and the treasuries confined their interest largely to an annual audit. The board of governors became a body corporate with full power, which it exercised directly in business matters and which it delegated to the president and the senate in academic matters.

[3]*House of Commons Debates*, May, 1918, p. 1999.
[4]O'Brien, *British Experiments in Public Ownership and Control*, pp. 96–7.

Tradition and practice varies, of course, among institutions, but responsibility and freedom have now been widely accepted as indispensable to efficient university teaching and management.

In the years since public trusts were first established the success of governmental participation in non-political activities has increased greatly. For this the trust form of administration must be given substantial credit since it brought to public administration the freedom, initiative, and business methods of private and personal enterprise and associated them with government rather than subordinated them to it. Without the public trust no legislature or department in a democratic state could possibly develop industries and resources, manage corporations, or create and spread ideas. There have been trouble and failure, of course, and the association of politics and business has not always been harmonious. Nevertheless, there have been invention and progress undreamed of by exponents of either public or private enterprise half a century ago.

The great exception to this trend in governmental administration is public school education. Here, despite all the public's experience in the areas of business and culture, power and responsibility have not been delegated but have been wielded directly by cabinets, ministers, departments, and municipal boards—with results that previous chapters have described. There is ample justification for suspecting that it is just this anomaly that causes most of the difficulties of the educational system, and may even account for the fact that general cultural progress has lagged so far behind economic progress. It seems obvious, therefore, that the time has long since come when the state should untie the political and bureaucratic apron strings and *trust* rather than run its schools.

I suggest that the state should try out the principle of the separation of ownership and control in education and the policy of establishing public schools as public trusts. I believe that a limited trial in a few schools would soon indicate the benefits of such a plan and lead to its gradual extension and finally general adoption. And I am strongly of the opinion that the public schools and their teachers would in the end amply justify the application to them of the same confidence which other institutions and professions in society now enjoy, so that education would become the vital and attractive field that it deserves to be. I therefore present the plan which follows. It is designed for a Canadian province, but it can be altered to suit the constitution of any other legislative unit.

The basic feature of the plan is the establishment as public trusts of large schools and "units" of small schools. "Central Memorial High School" would be created by statute as a publicly owned, body corporate managed by its own individual board of trustees which exercised its powers directly over business matters and which delegated powers over academic matters to a faculty council recognized and constituted by the creating statute. The trustees would have complete control over general policy and the property and finances of the school, all of which would be accounted for by annual audit and report. The faculty council would have full responsibility for the curriculum and services of the school, and would be accountable to the board through the principal. The latter would be responsible to the board of trustees in business matters and to the faculty council in academic matters. All curricular requirements, reports, and diplomas would be issued by, and in the name of, the school.

In the plan I am suggesting, the board of trustees of "Central Memorial" would consist of approximately ten members, including a chairman appointed by the board itself and the principal of the school *ex officio*. One-half of the trustees would be appointed by the provincial Council of Education (described below) and one-half by the local municipal council. Trustees would hold office for three years and be eligible for reappointment. No member of the provincial legislature, the cabinet, the civil service or of the local municipal council should be eligible to sit on the board. Its personnel should not be educationists, but laymen with general experience. They should not represent interest groups lest their minds be closed and their hands tied beforehand and lest they be forced to consider their personal affiliations ahead of the needs of the school. The board would appoint the principal and, upon his advice, appoint all other teachers and employees. One member of the board would be its treasurer who would keep strict account of all financial transactions according to the instructions of the board. The board would be required to make an annual report to the Council of Education, and its books would be subject to an annual audit by auditors appointed by the Council. There would be an executive committee of the board consisting of the chairman, the treasurer, and the principal which could, on authority of the board, handle items of business for which full meetings of the board would not be necessary. There is nothing unique, of course, about this type of administration; it is used in countless public and private organizations in every other field of endeavour.

The faculty council of "Central Memorial" would consist of its principal as chairman and members of its teaching staff to a number determined by the size of the school. Too large a council would get very little work done, and too small a one would not be sufficiently representative. If the school had a staff of thirty, for example, a council of twelve or so would be sufficient if it included the senior instructor in each of the departments of the school and, if desired, other members elected from among themselves by the teaching staff as a whole. The faculty council should appoint all committees of the staff, determine the curriculum for the school, and set out its own regulations and requirements concerning discipline, grading of pupils, and awarding of diplomas. The principal, as head of the school and chief executive officer of the board of trustees, would inform the council of the board's policies and of the business aspects of the school's management. In turn he would be advised by the faculty council and be its chief officer in all academic matters as well as its spokesman on the board of trustees. Like the head of any business concern he should be an effective liaison between those who decide and those who perform, be intimately concerned with the interests of both, and be reasonably responsible to both for his actions.

A careful division of jurisdiction would be necessary between the board of trustees and the faculty council, yet a free exchange of the ideas and opinions of each would be vital to the management of the school. Trustees are unfamiliar with the requirements of teaching, the sensibilities of teachers, and the attributes of pupils. Consequently, they should exercise only a very general control over policy and leave the details to the teachers who, individually and in faculty council, are best able to handle them. Teachers, in turn, are usually inexperienced in business matters, and they should act only in an advisory capacity in this field, leaving it mainly to the trustees who are responsible for balancing the budget.

The relations of these two bodies to the public are as important as those between themselves. The school is primarily an educational institution, and the people are chiefly interested in its teaching affairs. The staff and their principal, therefore, should be the spokesmen of the school to the public. The chairman and other members of the school board should remain in the background as do those of boards of hospitals, universities, railroads, and most corporations. The public should see, hear from, know, and be in direct contact with the school's teachers in relationships parallel with those in other enterprises. As in other institutions, however, those who speak for the school in public must scrupulously respect the policies of the board and the council.

There would, of course, still be a provincial authority with which each school or school unit had a connection and which would represent the general public interest. This provincial authority would be a Council of Education. The present office of minister and the department would be abolished and any existing power over educational funds held by the treasury department would be ended. The Council in a province of average size might consist of approximately twenty members. The chairman should be a layman of exceptional ability and prestige. He and one-half of the other members would be appointed by the provincial cabinet and the other half by the provincial teachers' federation. Members other than the chairman might be laymen or teachers, preferably half of each, but under no circumstances should they be members of the legislature or civil service. Members would hold office for three years and be eligible for reappointment, provided that no member served for more than three consecutive terms.

The Council of Education would have a staff of its own headed by a "Chief Adviser" or some such officer. It would be important to avoid terms such as "director," "superintendent," or "inspector," which imply domination, and this it is a purpose of the plan to remove. The employees of the Council would exercise staff functions only, and be available for advice, information, research, and consultation when requested either by the Council or by the schools. They would be appointed and paid by the Council itself, and under no circumstances should they be classified as civil servants.

The main functions of the Council would be two. First of all, it would determine the conditions under which schools might be designated public trusts and arrange for the administration of schools which cannot be so designated. The schools would then be organized and empowered by the legislature on the recommendation of the Council. Once a school was so "commissioned," however, the Council would have no control over its management unless intervention were requested by the school itself or by the municipality. Its second function would be the distribution of funds made available for education in the province. The Council would have a free hand in both fields, but it would report annually to the legislature through the Premier himself so that the report would have the best sponsorship in the House and run the least risk of interference from any department. The report would be published and widely circulated.

The financing of schools under this plan should be based on three general principles. (1) Schools may differ from many other public bodies in that they cannot finance themselves, but the state must let them handle the funds which are appropriated to them; they can manage these funds much better than a treasury. (2) Local authorities should be expected to pay their share of the costs. (3) Basic educational costs should take precedence over other public expenditures.

The funds made available by the province would first be appropriated by the legislature. The chairman of the Council of Education would present to the House through the Premier the annual budget of the Council. After the necessary discussion and explanation, and perhaps change, the budget would be approved and the Council would be given the entire sum to be banked in its own account. At the end of the fiscal year the Council would include in its annual report to the House a detailed audited financial statement showing how its revenue had been spent. A small portion of the funds would be used by the Council to defray its own expenses and to provide for agencies and services directly under its control, such as libraries, film boards, research bureaus, grants to cultural enterprises, and the like. The larger portion would be allocated among the schools according to a general formula. The agencies, services, and schools would, of course, submit annual budgets, reports, and financial statements to the Council in the same way as the Council would do to the legislature.

It is important to emphasize that accountability in financial matters should not imply subservience in policy; it would, of course, allow attention to obvious and flagrant abuse of funds. The legislature should be content to discuss and, if necessary, criticize the work of the Council, but it should refrain as far as possible from imposing its will through financial control over details of which it can really know very little and about which it cannot be expected to judge accurately. The Council, in turn, should adopt a similar policy in its relations with schools.

The Council, we have said, decides how to distribute the funds which the legislature has deemed the people of the province as a whole can afford as their share for education. This is a matter of major policy to be handled with great care. It would know at the outset that it could not please everybody but, after careful study it must make the decision alone and its decision must be final and binding. There are, of course, many factors upon the basis of which a formula could be determined: the population, nature, wealth, taxing power, and other features of localities; the number of pupils in localities and in schools; the number of teachers; the size and facilities of schools; and educational needs of various kinds. No one of these would be a sufficient determinant; the Council would have to combine them in a fashion which would, as accurately as possible, meet the demands of education itself and the financial resources and traditions of the province concerned. The next step is for the Council to determine how much each local administration *must* pay for the school or schools in its area. Perhaps, for example, the Council would provide enough to meet three-fifths of the cost of the basic educational needs of the schools in one town. The town's municipal council should then be expected to meet the other two-fifths. In some areas, of course, taxpayers are notoriously reluctant to pay school taxes, and there must therefore be some provision to ensure the performance of local obligations. This might be by statute. The legislature which wishes that all children have a basic minimum of instruction might well require in its municipal statutes that the local councils *must* pay their share as determined by the Council.

Here the principle of precedence of basic educational costs over other public expenditures might be made to prevail. Educational expenses can be considered as resembling food and rent in a family budget; they should be paid first and always in a public budget. An area that can, but will not finance its schools might well expect to have the school funds it will not give made available from provincial funds given for other services to the area. Why, for example, should a public paved highway in a district be built, maintained, and cleared of snow unless the local school is adequately financed? There may, of course, be objections that these are coercive methods and therefore not desirable; the right to an appropriate hearing of the local viewpoints before the Council will meet many of them. Where a district is really in difficulty the legislature would have to be prepared to enable the Council to meet all the basic costs of education in that area.

At this stage the Council of Education has determined how much basic costs should be in each school or unit and how much it and the local administrations should pay. There will, of course, be other expenses over and above the basic ones. Perhaps, for instance, the Council will not consider auditoriums, swimming pools, and certain vocational or other services in computing its grants. These would either be paid for by local sources or not be provided at all.

The management of a school should fit this broad financial arrangement. The board of trustees of "Central Memorial" would plan its annual budget, calculating the costs of maintaining the building and grounds, the teachers' salaries, the requirements for handling a certain number of pupils, and all other such items. It would submit this budget to the Council and the municipal authorities. It would learn from the Council exactly how much the total grant from all public sources would be, and it would receive the amount for deposit to its own account. It should also be able to receive funds from other private sources by way of endowments, gifts, grants, and the like. From this point on the detailed spending of the amount available should be entirely in the hands of the school.

It goes without saying that such a form of administration cannot be used at once, for all schools; it would have to be withheld from some institutions until they proved worthy of it by showing an efficient system of management. Nevertheless, the general principles are still applicable, even to the most remote one-room rural school. Here the form of administration should be the "unit" of schools, which has already been adopted in a limited way in some places. There may, for example, be twenty schools in a particular area, none of which could function as a trust by itself. The whole twenty would be organized in one trust with one board of trustees and one principal and faculty council for the group. The administration could then be carried on in the manner outlined above. As for an individual school which cannot for reasons of size or lack of competent staff be created a trust but which is not easily included in a group, it could be joined to an existing trust as an affiliated school, either permanently or until such time as it were ready to administer its own affairs.

Consider, for illustration, how the plan would appear in the "County of Woodboro." The county town may have two large, well-staffed school trusts, "Woodboro High School" and "St. Matthew's Elementary School." There may also be two small elementary schools. The latter, not big enough to be trusts, could be part of the "St. Matthew's" trust; the board would control them and the faculty council would include some of their teachers and direct their scholastic affairs. There may be five rural high schools in the county, four of which might be trusts, and one, near the town and too small to be a trust, which could be administered jointly with "Woodboro High." Twenty-five other rural schools might be joined in one trust. Thus, there would be seven trusts in all. The two urban schools would receive their revenue from the Council of Education and the town council according to whatever formulae prevailed, and, in addition, "Woodboro High" would receive revenue from local assessment for the rural high school attached to it. The four rural high school trusts and the unit trust would be financed from the Council and from local taxation in the districts in which they are situated. Like the county's churches, hospitals, and business firms, the school trusts, although supported by public funds, would be separate organizations, each with its own identity, governing body, and powers. The relationships among the trusts would be of their own making entirely. Administration would be in the hands of the schools, and responsibility for the education of the young people of the county would be clearly established as between the schools and the citizens.

Consider also how the business affairs of an individual school would be run. The board of "Woodboro High" would consist of a group of citizens interested in *this* school, *its* teachers, and *its* pupils. They would not be controlling an impersonal system of institutions and employees such as school trustees now control under the supervision of many and distant authorities and under conditions of almost pure routine. Rather they would have a school or unit with which they were directly connected and for which they were completely responsible. They would be encouraged to bring to their trusteeship personal interest, loyalty, and initiative, and it would obviously be more effective because it would mean more to them and to the school. Such a board could handle business matters far better than the present type because there would be an incentive to be business-like.

There would be checks in case of mismanagement. The most important would be the faculty council which, because it has status and powers of its own, is in a position to advise. Teachers would not and could not control the business of the school, but their opinions would be available and important to the board. The Council of Education would see the annual report, and it could warn the local board, either directly or through its auditors, of the possible consequences of mistaken policy. The local municipal council could also advise a board and its financial department could be in a position to render assistance if it were needed in an emergency. But these checks should be for emergency use only; the board should have every opportunity to be businesslike on its own.

Two aspects of business administration are involved. One is the handling of public funds in the public interest. A school should spend wisely any money which it receives from the taxpayers. In this respect a trust could go far beyond a mere government department or dependent board because it would be free to use the methods of business, to plan ahead, save, and invest for its own unit's needs, and would not be tied down by political whims and official rigidities in any of this. But the second aspect is equally important, though now almost completely ignored in schools: the administration of business as it concerns the unique interests and associations of the school itself. Just because education is a public service it does not follow that the details of its affairs should be *completely* determined by public standards of judgment because there are features of education which all the public cannot readily evaluate or understand. A board may, for example, want to try and find ways of going beyond the prevailing "public policy" of paying its teachers at clerical rates. It may see practical benefits in lawns and trees which the public has apparently ceased to expect near schools. It may be convinced that an adequate library will do better service to the school's pupils than an auditorium. It may want to give the arts and humanities as big a share of the school's budget as vocational facilities receive. In other words it should be permitted to run the school *as a school*, not wholly as a public institution. And this emphasis can actually have a practical side. Individuals and groups respect and assist organizations in inverse proportion to their public character. If the public associations of the school are over-emphasized, the government, which cannot do everything for it, will nevertheless be expected to do more and more for it. If, however, the school is able to build up an identity, character, and power of its own, it will command more public interest, respect, and help on its own than the government can command for it. As a result, donations may well be encouraged, and, more important, there would be developed in the public a more respectful attitude towards the schools and the teachers who work in them.

This business arrangement suggests a solution for a major educational problem in Canada—the fact that one government always finds it difficult to give financial assistance to another government's enterprises. Indeed, departments within one government often have trouble co-operating with one another in matters of finance. If school finance is removed from public finance and the politics which accompany the latter, and is identified instead with the schools themselves, the whole problem of "federal aid" and the like might well be solved. The federal government would, I suggest, find it much easier to give grants to a provincial Council of Education or, better still, directly to schools, than to a provincial government. It would be impossible, under such an arrangement, for a provincial government to use federal educational grants for purposes other than education and harder for it to cut down its own educational expenditure because of the grants. These practices have been followed in certain places; they throw doubt on the wisdom of federal grants and discourage almost entirely the giving of grants by other institutions and by individuals. The consolidated revenue fund, the quicksand into which so many educational funds have disappeared or by which so many have been kept away, should, therefore, be replaced in education (as it is in most other public enterprises) by funds and budgets administered for schools rather than for governments.

A further advantage of the trust form of administration is the incentive to progress. When every school shares a common pot and functions without a budget and funds of its own, there is no real spur to efficiency in any school and the whole system is soon managed sloppily. If one school needs a new furnace, it should not have to await completion of a roof in another school; a salary raise in one place should not be blocked because it cannot be given somewhere else; if one school saves some of its funds after the fiscal year ends, other schools should have no share of them. As individual trusts, the more businesslike schools would have every scope for their efforts and would not be kept to the pace of the slowest; the weaker ones at the beginning would have to become more businesslike because they would be on their own without someone else pulling them along in half-hearted fashion, and because their inefficiencies would be emphasized to their detriment by the progress and prestige of better-organized schools.

I am quite aware that such a plan will have immediately raised certain objections and questions. Some at least of these can be anticipated and should now be examined.

The responsibility of schools to the people is a fundamental matter. Can public school trusts be more responsible than legislatures, cabinets, and departments of education? I believe they can because they would be closer to both education and the people, and because they would not be hampered by the weaknesses in the field of education of political institutions. The Council of Education would have far more time for, and direct interest in education than any branch of government: it could be more readily advised and informed by school authorities; it would not have to worry about the effects of its actions on votes and political promotion; it would have enough power to influence but not enough to meddle; its services would always be available, yet schools would not be too dependent on it. The school trusts would be more responsible than either governments or existing schools: they would be created at a central level, but run on a local level; they would not merely be branches of some distant department whose "responsibility" is more apparent than real, but respected units with something of their own to do and a real interest of their own in their community; they can be close to public opinion, yet they can be in a position to withstand uninformed or selfish pressures. There would not be, indeed there could not be, any diminishing of the sovereignty of the legislature.

Rather there would be the recognition that the power to legislate in educational matters, as in other fields, does not require the exercise of direct powers of control, but the delegation of these powers to responsible institutions associated with, but not dominated by, the government.

A well-known passage on this subject applies perfectly to the educational system:

There can be little doubt that on the whole the relinquishment by Parliament of its detailed day-to-day "control" over the undertakings run by public boards is an immense advantage. . . . Parliament is an excellent instrument for the formulation of new policy in legislative terms, but it is much less effective in supervising administration of a complex character. . . . The most conspicuous fact . . . is the depressing effect on departmental initiative and administrative energy of continual liability to parliamentary inquisition on points of minor detail. An excessive caution becomes the indispensable passport to eminence in official life when even a slight deviation from established routine may land the minister in a quagmire of unforseen difficulties. Routine, precedent, and the avoidance of risks tend to become the navigating lights by which the departmental ship is steered.

The result of this enervating discipline may be of no great consequence in a well-developed or fully mature field of activity in which most of the work is of a routine character. But in new or growing spheres of activity the whole tempo of administration is likely to be slowed down or even stopped entirely.[5]

Those who think of responsibility in terms of finance may wonder how or why taxpayers' money should be spent by anyone outside the control of the public treasury. Actually treasury departments are really accounting and auditing offices, and they are quite incapable of either determining how money should be spent or spending it. "A treasury," wrote Mr. Clement Attlee, "is not really concerned with economy but with parsimony."[6] This difficulty is perfectly illustrated by the gross inefficiencies of education finance as it operates under direct government control, and it is the main reason why treasury control has been limited in other fields in most countries. "Rigid control of expenditure by the Treasury," writes one authority, "puts initiative and willingness to assume non-insurable risk at a discount, a deadening influence upon any organiza-

[5]Robson, *Public Enterprise*, pp. 377–8.
[6]C. R. Attlee, "The Bridgeman Committee Report," *Public Administration*, X (Oct. 1932), p. 352.

tion not concerned with purely routine operations."[7] "The absence of Treasury control of the traditional kind," writes another, "is wholly desirable. . . . The Treasury is, therefore, not merely of little use as a controlling agent over the finance of public boards but likely to be positively detrimental to their future development."[8]

How, it will be asked, can co-ordination of curriculum, standards, and teaching be assured and confusion avoided? I would repeat that the present centralized system neither assures co-ordination nor prevents confusion because the prevailing standards are artificial. Moreover it impedes progress because co-ordination created by officials from above unfortunately tends to become fixed; once a measure of it is achieved it has to be maintained: the result can only be called conformity.

One might go on and ask how far co-ordination is a desirable goal at all. It has been stressed in previous pages that what is needed and what is practical is only a partial co-ordination, a kind of proceeding in the right direction rather than a maintenance of a standard speed and the reaching of a set goal. A profession and those it serves can realize this partial co-ordination; a government cannot. A government could have registered Toscanini and me in the same course in music, but nothing it could do would co-ordinate our efforts; it could place J. P. Morgan and Company and Joe's Pawn Shop under common regulations but not be able to guarantee that their services would be in any way co-ordinated. Moreover, the greater the co-ordination in these instances, the more Toscanini and J. P. Morgan's and those served by them would suffer. If, however, it should be desired that my musical efforts be somehow related to Toscanini's or that some standard be determined between Joe's and J. P. Morgan's a logical comparison could only be made on the basis of Joe's and my efforts to raise our standards of achievement, and of the recognition afforded by musicians and concert-goers in the one instance and business men and customers in the other. The same is true of schools, teachers, and pupils: programmes representing govern-

[7]Lincoln Gordon, *The Public Corporation in Great Britain* (London: Oxford, 1938), p. 321.
[8]Robson, *Public Enterprise,* p. 383.

mental co-ordination and recognition of standards mean little compared with the actual work done by them, and only the people directly concerned can exercise reasonable judgments on this work. Although complete co-ordination is unobtainable, most people want some assurance that schools are following a common programme so that, for instance, grade eight in one place can reasonably be compared with grade eight somewhere else. Previous pages have described how difficult such an arrangement is under centralized, artificial co-ordination. I believe that much more reasonable standards could be developed if the schools and the teaching profession had the same freedom to control their work that every other group from carpenters to architects have in theirs. Medical practice furnishes one comparison. There are many standards which hospitals and doctors have recognized and followed on their own, even through the many changes which have taken place in medicine in the last ten years; and there is infinitely more real co-ordination among them than there is in educational circles. It was not departments of health which brought this happy situation about, but the profession itself. Engineering is another example: if it had to await the guidance and promptings of departments of public works, society would still be in the age of the wigwam and dugout canoe. Co-ordination, or rather the amount of it that is necessary to prevent confusion and permit progress, should therefore be a professional concern.

If schools became public trusts, they and the teaching profession could develop such standards as are required. Standards would depend not on artificial elements revealing the imposition of undesirable uniformity but on the real elements—the efforts of individuals and the demands of subjects. Schools, like banks and insurance companies, would know what was going on in other institutions. Able mathematics or history teachers would then, like distinguished leaders in other fields, be able to influence standards and set examples among their colleagues. Teachers' associations and publications, like business and professional organizations and literature, would encourage the exchange of ideas and practices. The demands of English and arithmetic, like those of wiring houses or making dentures, would be interpreted by the group concerned and met by those who benefit from them. None of these relationships operates in education today: schools have little contact with one another; leaders are rare in the teaching profession; existing journals or publications do not enable teachers to keep in direct touch with new developments in subjects or with what other teachers are doing; new knowledge takes a long time to percolate through the school system. The obstruction is complete dependence on officialdom; the remedy is the release of personal initiative and professional respect.

Will schools not differ from one another under a trust system? They will, and why should they not? They are different now—anyone who thinks regulations make a badly taught grade eight the same as a well taught one is singularly optimistic. Official regulations and labels only serve to disguise the difference and perpetuate it in an unhealthy form. Consequently, *desirable* difference should be encouraged. For instance, if one school wants to start French in grade two and has the staff to do so, why obstruct it because other schools cannot? If one school considers the English curriculum inadequate, a history text poor, the fashion of teaching mathematics unsuitable, should it not be allowed to improve them, even if its programme then differed from those of other schools? The results might well be so satisfactory that other schools would follow the example set. Twenty years ago every doctor kept mothers in bed two weeks after childbirth; some, despite protest, tried getting them up within a few days; now all follow the new method. Every school subject and teaching practice could benefit from the same process if it were allowed to operate. More important, however, is the bringing of existing difference out into the open. Today the inadequacies of poor schools and teachers are well hidden; not only is the public uninformed about them, but there is also no incentive for them to change and little freedom for good schools and teachers to strike out on their own. Under a trust system good teaching would receive a needed stimulus because it would be known and recognized, and bad teaching would suffer so much by comparison that improvement would be forced, not by regulation, but by professional and public opinion. Some will cry that pupils will not all "get" the same thing and reach the same level on leaving school. They do not now; and why should they? But would a system of trusts thereby be "undemocratic"? Emphatically not, because it would encourage a healthy, stimulating development of individual initiative and responsibility which, surely, is one of the chief requirements of democracy.

Doubt may also arise concerning protection against inefficient administration. Who is to guarantee that "Woodboro High" will be managed properly and what will happen if it is not? It is of course no answer, however true, to say that there are no reliable guarantees that a school is managed properly at the present time, and that there are many schools functioning today under conditions that would not be tolerated in other activities. It is, however, my conviction that management would be infinitely better if the present form of external administration by outside officials were replaced with a trust system of internal administration by persons directly and intimately associated with the schools. Budgeting, planning, ordering, and spending would mean far more if they had to be clearly understood because they were directly handled by the school. And not only would wasteful extravagance be easily located but undue parsimony would also be readily recognized. Officials would be on tap, not on top, and the dangers of too much administration restricting teaching would be greatly lessened. If any weak places in the system appeared and if any school were managed badly there could be no buck-passing among politicians, officials, trustees, teachers, and taxpayers—one of the chief troubles today. Responsibility would be clearly established with the board, teachers, and taxpayers of the local school concerned. But what would happen to a school that could not run itself and to the pupils in its district? Suppose, for instance, that today a school's trustees cannot or will not pay its teacher; it asks for, and gets, an untrained teacher with no qualifications and its pupils get third-rate instruction. Under a trust arrangement the community would either pay for a qualified teacher, as it does for a clergyman or a doctor, or it would do without a teacher. Such a situation would not occur very often before local taxpayers would pay more to teachers than to potato diggers and road workers, and realize that the local school, like the church, hospital, and store, is not just a service to be automatically demanded regardless of quality, but an institution to be respected and managed properly. This happy situation can only be brought about by full and direct local responsibility. It is true that there may be local difficulties which are real and unavoidable; in these cases however, the Council of Education can make special arrangements; in emergencies it would be in a far better position than government to combine local resources and educational requirements.

Some people may comment in reply to this presentation that there is already a certain amount of decentralization in some school systems, and indeed various authorities have advocated more of it. "I hope," wrote a retiring Superintendent of Schools in Vancouver in his final annual report to his superior, "that you and your associates in your Department will endeavour to see that autonomy within each of the school districts of this Province will be extended and not curtailed. To assure that British Columbia will continue to lead in the field of education in Canada it is essential that democracy be allowed to function in the school districts themselves."[9] But the concept of decentralization presently fashionable and alluded to here implies that the central authority will *allow* the local authorities to do more and give scope to the activities of regional officials. This type of decentralization cannot bring lasting improvement: the local powers must *belong* to the school, and the school, *its* authorities, and *its* teachers should exercise *their* powers.

I have been asked what would happen under this plan to the large number of people now holding positions as departmental officials and school inspectors and superintendents. I have discussed this point with several of them and have asked two questions of them: is there really anything the administrators now do that cannot be handled more

[9]H. N. MacCorkindale in *Annual Report of the Superintendent of Education for the Province of British Columbia*, 1953–4, p. 55.

effectively by school officers? Would not the conscientious official be happier as a teacher or as a combined teacher and administrator in a school than he is in the provincial or municipal civil service? The answers I have received have convinced me that the administrators would have more useful and happier careers if those among them who can teach were to rejoin the teaching profession and if those among them who wished to remain administrators only were transferred to other departments in the government service.

British experiences illustrate the application of some features of this plan, although the public trust is not yet established in the British state educational system. At the top there is a completely different outlook from that in North American governments. "In this country," says the British Minister of Education, "we have a system of education headed by a Minister whose duty it is to avoid interference in matters of curriculum, provided by local authorities who would be quick to resent interference with their independence, and manned by a teaching profession very jealous of its academic freedom."[10] This policy permits the operation of 146 separate local education authorities, each dealing with different types of schools. Anything like centralization in Whitehall, "uniform" standards, and curriculum control in the North American sense is unknown. Yet while county or municipal autonomy in educational matters is an advantage over central control, it is still not enough. County and municipal administration is governmental and it is subject to all the vagaries of politics. Responsible local autonomy must rest in the schools themselves even where they are wholly owned and financed by the state.

This viewpoint is accepted by many authorities in Britain as it applies to academic policy in the schools. The most respected British schools are those in which freedom is valued most, in which the school boards and staffs are left by the local education authorities to manage their own curriculum and teaching matters. Financial autonomy is a rarer policy. When I inquired about it on a recent

[10]Lord Hailsham before the annual meeting of the Association of Education Committees, Brighton, June 1957; *Education*, June 28, 1957, p. 1197.

tour of Britain, I found that some schools enjoy a good deal of it in practice, although such a happy privilege cannot be publicly acknowledged. For an open and liberal policy in this respect I was urged frequently to go to Hertfordshire. I did so, and found that since April, 1950, headmasters of schools there have had substantial financial freedom in the purchasing of supplies and the handling of ordinary running expenses. "A bank account is opened for each school," says the County Treasurer in a published statement, "fed by the County Treasurer by instalments . . . mainly on a capitation basis." "The Head," he added, "may order supplies from whatever source he wishes and he pays all the bills himself by drawing cheques on the account. . . . He may spend the money on items covered by the allowance in any proportion he thinks fit. Furthermore, if he has a balance unspent at the end of the financial year he may carry it forward for use in the next year."[11]

This system has worked extremely well, and it has greatly increased both the efficiency and the self-respect of the schools concerned. Although it is limited to ordinary running expenses it is still a privilege of which most state schools could only dream and on which most departments of education and school boards in North America would look with horror as an encroachment on their sacred prerogatives. Yet schools are the only institutions which must do without such a privilege. The wonder is not that they do not have it, but that it is not extended much further so that *all* school funds are handled directly by school authorities, that staff are paid by the school's cheques, and that the school's budget and business methods may be directed responsibly and efficiently. The school staffs will not go on sprees with their funds; they are just as worthy of responsibility as are the staffs of any other institutions.

I have been describing a method of school administration which does not exist in North American public schools today as the basis for what is needed to remedy both obvious and hidden weaknesses. What the results of an implementation of the trust system would be can only be a matter of opinion until it is tried out. Numerous other

[11]Hertfordshire County Council Bulletin, *The School General Account* (Hertford, 1956), p. 3.

policies, projects, and reforms have been tried, and still public schooling is in a state of turmoil and teaching is not attractive to enough people of the required calibre. I suggest that now the trust should be given a fair trial. It should not be introduced too quickly or too extensively but it should be tested in a few schools, as it was in industrial and cultural activities long ago. A legislature, in co-operation with some municipalities, might set up a Council of Education and establish several school trusts on a trial basis. I believe that the most serious problem would be a welcome one: the conditions of administration would be so much improved in the school trusts that teachers and pupils would be eagerly seeking admission to them rather than to the older type of school and parents and local authorities would be requesting extension of the plan.

Administration of schools, however, is only one aspect of education, and the secondary one. The other is teaching, including the training and licensing of teachers, their conditions of work, and the powers of their profession. The trust plan, indeed any reform of the school system, will not work by improved administration alone; it will have to be accompanied by improved status for the teachers, their work, and their profession.

8. Freedom
to Teach

THE PUBLIC SCHOOL TRUST, AS IT IS BEING SUGGESTED IN THESE PAGES, is organized around the principle of the freedom to teach. This principle should be established in the conditions of work in schools and in the manner and matter of teaching itself, the training and licensing of teachers, and the status of teachers' organizations. Freedom to teach is a necessary accompaniment for ability to teach because it liberates judgment and initiative. Freedom is also essential to professional respect: self-respect among teachers is required if their ambitions are to find satisfaction in teaching; the respect of the public is vital if teaching is to be recognized as a profession worthy of the support we say it deserves. Any doctor, lawyer, or newspaper man would say the same of his occupation. It is time that our society realized that the training of the mind requires conditions of freedom at least as favourable as those applicable in the treatment of the body, the practice of law, and the reporting of daily news. The suggestions made in this chapter about freedom to teach are necessarily very general. The details involved will be seen as a result of study and discussion in the schools and the teaching profession.

For the system being outlined here, it would first have to be established that what goes on in the classrooms of a school is primarily the business of that school and the teaching profession. The responsibility under such an arrangement is clear: the profession would control the licensing of teachers and participate in their training; the boards of trustees would have the power to appoint the teachers on advice from their staffs; and the faculty councils of the schools and the teachers themselves would be in charge of the curriculum and the teaching.

The conditions of teaching in a school would thereupon be changed substantially. The curriculum of "Central Memorial" would be entirely in the hands of its faculty council which would determine the subjects to be taught, the standards required of its pupils, the certification given to them, and other such matters. The board of trustees would recognize and accept the council's power and interest itself in academic matters only where the budget was affected or where serious difficulties arose which the council could not solve. Thus the programme of a school would be decided, not in a remote government office, but in the board room of the school by the group of people who best know their subjects and pupils, who have the most realistic grasp of conditions, and who are in closest touch with the standards that both universities and employers require.

The faculty council would meet regularly under the chairmanship of the principal. It would take up in free and open discussion all matters affecting the academic activities of the school, and bring forth the advice and criticism of any teacher about any activity, course or regulation. Most important of all, the council would *decide*, something which teachers' meetings cannot do now because they lack any real power. Under such an arrangement there would no longer be any excuse for lack of interest or buck-passing because the responsibility and the power to exercise it would be clearly vested and recognized. There would be ample scope for the discussion, and perhaps implementation, of new ideas and procedures, the recognition of different viewpoints, and the exchange of advice between the staff and the board of trustees each of which has something to contribute to the other. As a result the school could be a living organization with a sense of unity in its own particular duty and a pride in exercising it; inevitably these would be reflected both in the zeal of its teachers and in the quality of their work.

The great advantage of this plan is the determination of the curriculum according to the demands of the subjects to be taught, the facilities of the school, the abilities of the pupils, and the standards of the profession. The hampering influence of weaker schools and of the dead provincial "average" would be removed and the school and its pupils could forge ahead on their own. The example of stronger schools could be a real influence on others because it could operate and be seen to operate free from the present cloak of official "common" standards. The school, like any other organization, would have to depend on its own qualities and reputation and there could be none of the covering-up of weaknesses or of strengths so general today. The success of mathematical instruction, for instance, would depend directly on the teachers and it would no longer be so easy to fulfil general requirements applicable to good and bad teaching alike; there would soon be no doubt as to whether the school could teach mathematics or not. It would not take long for employers, universities, pupils, and parents to recognize the merits of different schools, because relative competence upon graduation, now completely disguised, would soon be traceable to particular schools and teachers. The schools badly need this kind of stimulus to good teaching, and it can only be secured by giving them direct responsibility.

A more realistic relation between the curriculum and the quality of the teachers would be another beneficial result. A school which offered courses and facilities would have a clear understanding of, and obvious responsibility for, the type of teaching staff required. "Any teacher" will not do; if a school offers five years of French, for example, that announcement will be a promise to teach pupils properly in that language, and the school will have to seek a teacher who knows the subject. Moreover, passing someone else's 50 per cent standard will not do for the pupils; the school would either teach French or it would not and the result will be obvious because the responsibility is direct.

For the teachers, control of the curriculum would thus provide a new and stimulating interest in their work. They could plan their own courses, set their own requirements, and use the texts and materials which they and others found most suitable. They would have a sense of personal responsibility which would not only improve their work but also make teaching an attractive occupation, not for clerks, but for those who respect both knowledge and young people. The "do what you're told" atmosphere would be replaced by a policy of allowing teachers to do what they think best in the light of professional standards—the only policy upon which good teaching can really be based.

Once the faculty has determined the curriculum and requirements, individual teachers should be free to teach their courses as they see fit. Miss Jones of "Central Memorial," teaching history in grade eleven, would follow, not a rigid programme, worked out at a distance from her classroom, but a plan determined by and for herself. She would know, from consultation with her colleagues, what was taught in grade ten and what will be expected in grade twelve; she would know what other history teachers in other schools were doing; she could find out the various amounts of knowledge already achieved by her pupils; she could select what she thinks is the best of the available textbooks; and she could plan exactly the course to be followed and the special assignments for fast and slow pupils.

There would, of course, have to be co-ordination among teachers. It would be more effective under such an arrangement than under the present system of artificial requirements. No departmental rule that page 205 shall mark the end of grade ten and the beginning of grade eleven can compare with actual co-operation among teachers in any one school in providing orderly progress for pupils. Likewise, co-ordination among schools should and could be a matter for teachers to handle through their professional associations and personal contacts.

Better teaching on the whole is surely to be expected under a trust plan. Inexperienced or incompetent teachers will not be able to rely on following official formulas; they will have to find out how to keep up with other teachers and meet professional standards. Today it is very hard to recognize the differences between a poor teacher and a good one because of the mechanics of a common curriculum which are easily "covered" by the one and which hold back the other, and because the standards set are governmental and arbitrary, not professional. Indeed, teachers themselves rarely recognize each other's merits because they do not have to pay any attention to them, and there are few leaders in the sense of professional recognition of competence. With freedom to teach, the good teacher is on her own and, like a competent surgeon, solicitor, or preacher, stands forth as a living example to her contemporaries more effective than even the most carefully planned rule book. Pupils will know the difference as soon as the hobbles are removed from their teachers; parents will soon hear of Miss Smith's superiority; employers will recognize that the best prepared pupils come from certain schools and teachers; and the laggards in the profession will soon be jolted out of their lethargy and inefficiency. The emphasis on talent and achievement could be the biggest single factor in making teaching sufficiently attractive to hold those who are now leaving by the thousands and to encourage the many others who would like to teach but who go to other fields where talent is recognized and encouraged.

Under such an arrangement the principal of the school need not be immersed in tasks resembling those of a file clerk and a floor walker. As chief executive officer of the board of trustees he would need to see that the board's policy is followed and that the school's business affairs are handled according to the budget established. As chairman of the faculty council he would direct the school according to the academic policy determined by the council. Furthermore, once the control of a government department is removed, the principal can think of himself as a possible leader in his profession and a scholar, and not as someone else's agent; the headship of a school would be a professional attainment in itself and not a stepping-stone to administration outside the school.

The improvement of conditions of work by the freedom to teach would inevitably have to be accompanied by increased salaries. There is no sense in pious recommendations that salaries be increased unless there is justification for the increase; and that justification will only come if good teaching is publicly recognized and respected. There is surely a reason related to prestige for the low level of teachers' salaries; it is not always because the taxpayers are niggardly or the treasuries are empty. States paying enormous sums for munitions and highways, and individuals paying lavishly for personal services and amusements, should not be guilty of discrimination against teachers. People respect and pay those who have some power or reveal some special talent in the dispensing of their services. Teachers as a class are neither respected nor paid satisfactorily because they have no power which will enable them to bring forward their profession, so that the many talented teachers are not sufficiently recognized and the too many uneducated and incompetent people in the profession hold back the others. The law of supply and demand should be permitted to operate in the paying of teachers. Government interference now keeps it from operating by the imposition of a rigid classification system. Consequently, the supply of teachers remains desperately short and salaries are prevented from going up enough to adjust supply to demand. Yet the operation of the law in other occupations draws numerous teachers to them. Salaries, therefore, should be left to the trustees and the profession, as they are to employers and professions in other vocations.

Under the trust system being proposed, the first factor in the determination of salaries within a school would be a schedule of positions and salaries drawn up by arrangement between the board of trustees and the faculty council. Promotion within this schedule would be strictly a matter for the board, the principal, and the individual teacher concerned and the schedule itself should be flexible enough to enable the school to hire and retain the best available personnel. The second factor would be the ability of the individual teachers: every opportunity for rapid promotion would be encouraged so that competence and devotion to duty could be rewarded. The third factor would be the market for individual teachers: if mathematicians are scarce and English teachers numerous, the former will have to be paid more; if one school pays higher salaries than another, the latter will have to adjust its scale or do without. These factors should result in a healthy adjustment of teachers' salaries to the demands of their work and to salaries in other occupations.

There are, of course, many teachers and trustees today who do not like "merit rating," and who emphasize only seniority, hours of work, and credits in training schools. They need to remember that no other profession relies on these criteria alone, and that ability must be recognized above all else if teaching is to be respected and paid. Teachers' fear of the possible prejudice of trustees and principals is no more justified than fear of an employer, bank manager, regimental commander, or anyone else who pays or recommends for promotion. Certainly it should be far less of an obstacle than the impersonal computations of distant politicians and civil servants and the hampering influence of incompetent teachers who hold back the able. A recognized practice with a necessary degree of flexibility would, under conditions of freedom, gradually evolve and it would be bound to result in the end in generally higher salaries.

Those who fear that schools will compete with one another for teachers should ask themselves "Why not?" Hospitals, business firms, and individual employers compete for services and those whom they employ are, without exception, paid better than teachers. Actually competition for teachers' services does go on: it may not be among the schools themselves, but every other vocation competes with the schools with obviously disastrous results.

The quality of teachers must, of course, be improved greatly before the freedom to teach can be fully justified. Both the schools and the profession must disavow the commonly held idea that anyone can teach and repudiate the emphasis on methods which has done so much to lower the qualifications required. The practice of recruiting teachers from the lower half of graduating classes must end before any substantial improvement can take place in the schools, and before the profession can expect to acquire proper respect from the public. Good teachers are not found, of course, only among the top scholars; but no one should be permitted to teach unless he has made at least second class standing in his own studies—surely a logical requirement—and anyone in the third class group who thinks he has a "flair" for teaching should improve his own standing before setting forth to instruct others.

Two things should be clearly understood in relation to the new system being proposed. The fitness to teach should be determined by the quality of a candidate's work—not just the number of courses taken. A young lady with a good record at the sophomore level will make a better teacher (other things being equal) than another with two years of mediocre achievement and some further credits achieved with third class standing. Secondly, the primary emphasis should be on courses concerned with the subjects which the candidate will teach, and methods should be studied in connection with these subjects. The situation revealed by the Ontario Association of Professional Engineers in which 400 out of 630 teachers of mathematics and science in Ontario high schools were found to have taken no courses in these subjects beyond the high school level, bears dramatic testimony to the need for this change of emphasis.

All teacher training, it is suggested, should be handled in universities and junior colleges of recognized standing whose standards are acceptable to the teaching profession. Separate normal schools would be abolished and control by political officials ended. Under such an arrangement teacher trainees would no longer be a group apart screened off from other students by political auspices and confined to a narrow programme encouraging methodological inbreeding and with special low standards all its own. They would have access to courses on equal terms with other students and would enjoy the benefits of the influences and associations which only a university can give; surely those are immensely desirable for those who would devote a lifetime to learning and teaching. The standing of the university is vitally important in this scheme and only those universities which are worthy of the name should prepare teachers. Institutions which are but glorified high schools and whose degrees are worth little more than matriculation certificates (there are several of them) should not be permitted to train teachers. There is nothing very novel in this arrangement: it simply applies to teaching the same direction of professional education by universities which already prevails in other fields.

Within the university the training of teachers would be in the hands of an educational council of the faculty of arts and science. This would be a radical change because it would mean a much closer contact between university departments and school teaching than now exists. Indeed, the lack of such contact is undoubtedly one of the reasons for the present playing-down of academic attainment as a requirement for teacher training. The authorities who license teachers have hitherto dealt almost exclusively with faculties of "education"; and professors in the arts and science subjects have largely ignored school teaching because there has been no incentive to develop an interest on their own part and no consultation of them by authorities.

This barrier between schools and universities cannot be justified. It is harmful to both because schools do not have association with leaders in the various fields of knowledge, and the universities do not have sufficient opportunity to influence the preparation of their prospective students. Again, mathematics furnishes a good example; by the time a young person reaches the university it is too late for the latter to do much for him in that subject if he has not already secured a substantial grounding in it in school. In this, and indeed in all basic subjects, sustained contact between university teachers and school teachers would be invaluable for the work of both.

The abolition of separate faculties of "education" would be essential to this contact. They stand at present between the arts and science departments and both the authorities and the schools; they are controlled by governmental rather than educational authorities; and they tend to feature methodology and theory at the expense of knowledge of subjects. It is necessary to face the fact that pedagogy, the technique of teaching, should be considered only along with study of the subjects to be taught. It cannot be abandoned: we should remember that teaching subject-matter to prospective teachers is not enough in itself; they need instruction in how to teach the subjects and in this university departments must be prepared to take more interest than they do now.

The purpose of the educational council of the faculty of arts and science being suggested would be, therefore, the long-overdue joining of pedagogy and learning. It would include representatives of departments whose subjects are taught in schools; and all of them should either have or secure knowledge of and contact with the teaching of their subjects in the schools. Each department would arrange, under the direction of the educational council, special lectures or seminars on the techniques of teaching its subject and on the fundamentals which comprise the school course in it. Many departments have professors who are excellent teachers themselves and who know the activities of the schools; those not so fortunate could secure the part-time services of skilled high school teachers to undertake this special work.

Professors of "education" as such, who today are really instructors in general methodology, would no longer be found. All those instructing in the art of teaching would first be professors in a department; second, they would also be members of the educational council. No one would be instructing in teaching unless he were of sufficient standing in some subject to be teaching that subject as well as teaching prospective teachers how to teach. Under such an arrangement the educational council would be merely a co-ordinating and administrative body. It would give no courses of its own for credit: its function would be to co-ordinate the pedagogical work of the departments, give special series of lectures if required, maintain contact with teachers' associations and with their requirements for teacher training, and arrange for apprenticeship in the schools.

The present courses and degree programmes in "education," including postgraduate work, would be broken up and the essential part of their contents distributed among the departments concerned. The department of history, for example, would then instruct in the teaching of history. Furthermore, general matters such as the history, philosophy, and psychology of education could be assigned to the departments of history, philosophy, and psychology which could provide special instruction and reading and research for those who wish to do special work in these subjects. It would then be (as it should be) the department of psychology which would supervise study in "correlates of attitudes among clinical psychology students" and a department of political science which would direct a thesis on "the log cabin symbol in American presidential politics," and not a teachers' college as at present. Those who fear that pedagogical studies would become too academic under academic teachers might pause to wonder why Columbia Teachers' College gives doctor's degrees in education for theses on "the effects of alcohol on fear extinction" and "the political views of the eighteenth-century New England clergy as expressed in their election sermons."[1] Each of the thirty-six doctoral dissertations enumerated in the list from which these samples were taken is more appropriate to university departments concerned with subjects than to a department of "education."

The university then, would determine the fitness of candidates to teach the subjects offered in the schools. For instruction in school law, methods, practice teaching, and the like, we must turn to the teaching profession and the schools.

Internship and practice of the type which prevails in law, medicine, and theology would in the plan being outlined replace the present ineffective lectures by professional "educators" and sp asmodic visits to model schools. This training could be handled in various ways depending on the locality and the candidates themselves. A young man preparing for teaching could, while he is still at university, be given useful full-time training in a school during the months of September, May, and June when schools are open and colleges are closed, and he could be assigned a regular schedule of visits during the remainder of the year for the purpose of observing and teaching. The marking of exercises, essays, book reviews, and the like is a useful training for the student; school teachers could assign more of such work to pupils and thus ease their own burden of time-consuming correcting. Special tutoring of both bright and slow pupils,

[1] See *Teachers' College Record*, January, 1957, pp. 233–5.

assistance in high school science laboratories, observing seat work in primary classes, handling small groups in conversational French, and helping with physical training and manual training are just a few functions which would give experience to student teachers and much needed help to the schools. School administration and regulations, curriculum requirements, and the like can best be handled through introducing the student to them in the schools and assigning reading about them. They are not worthy of special courses. General literature on such subjects is available in university libraries and students with special interests could readily be referred to them. The school should have the same responsibility for seeing that its junior teachers become familiar with the essentials of this kind as law and engineering firms, banks, insurance companies, hospitals, churches, and universities have respecting similar matters in their fields.

A third party would share the responsibility of preparing young teachers: the teaching profession itself. Without its participation the plan under discussion will not work. A teachers' organization would co-operate with the university councils which certify teachers and with the schools which give them apprenticeship. Moreover, it would give the qualifying examinations needed for licensing, and thus co-ordinate the efforts of the other two groups. It would accept the verdicts of the universities on the broad training candidates had received through college courses and of the school authorities on achievement in practice; it would itself examine on the specific material to be taught. This last is important because advanced training is no guarantee that a student will know the actual material he will teach in the school. There are many "qualified" teachers in schools today who have not mastered what they are teaching and can proceed only by textbook. The certificate of the profession, clearly setting forth the courses taken and class of standing of the candidate, would be the official licence to teach. Again there is the obvious parallel with the successful experience of other professions.

In discussing this plan of apprenticeship with others, I have been reminded that similar schemes have failed in the past. They have, but for one reason: they lacked professional auspices and leadership.

Apprenticeship implies association with senior members of a craft who, in the interest of the craft, share their knowledge and experience with beginners. The intern, the articled law clerk, and the carpenter's helper are trained under this kind of association. But apprenticeship has not been like this in the public schools. The departments and superintendents have arranged it; governmental regulations have determined its nature; and the profession and the craft have had a minor, if indeed any place in the arrangements. Apprenticeship in pedagogy can only be successful if it is controlled by the teaching profession itself.

Here, then, is a combination of college training and professional control of specific material and methods, each arranged by those best qualified to do so. Two present weaknesses are thus met. First, it will take care of those who have a flair for handling young people but who are not particularly well educated, since all will be instructed at the better universities; and it will take care of those who are well educated but do not understand teaching since there will be guidance by schools and the profession. The teachers who result from the process will not all be perfect any more than are all members of other professions, but the combination of knowledge and teaching skill achieved should be in better balance than it is today. The second weakness which will be countered is the bureaucratic control of officials who do not teach, who do not know the candidates, whose professional attachments are purely incidental, and whose interests are too close to politics. The termination of their control would be one of the chief means of liberating teacher training from mediocrity.

Two typical cases will illustrate the process. Mary Jones wants to teach school and she plans to take one year in university, perhaps the minimum period required before she can get a licence. She must first have completed her matriculation with at least second class standing. She will apply to a recognized university for admission and to her provincial teachers' organization for registration as a student teacher. The teachers' organization may assign her to one of the schools in her locality to help and observe during the period between the opening of school and registration day at university; and, with the co-operation of the university, associate her with a school or schools in the city in which the university is located. She will register in the university, fulfil the usual requirements for the freshman year in arts or science, and take the regular classes and examinations.

She will probably be taking English, history, French, mathematics, and a science. Each of the departments concerned will be offering special classes in the techniques of teaching its subject, and Mary will take these classes. This work will not be "extra" because it will serve as a useful review of the fundamentals which she may or may not have grasped when she was in school herself. In the mathematics department, for example, a skilled mathematician who understood school teaching would show her how to teach vulgar fractions intelligently, how to do mental arithmetic, how to make algebra interesting, and the like. At the end of the year Mary's record as a student will be assessed in the usual way by the registrar's office and it must reveal at least second class standing. In addition the educational council of faculty comprising the instructors from each department who gave the special classes in the technique of teaching will assess her record and abilities on the information of the instructors under whom she sat for these classes. A fairly accurate report of Mary's academic qualifications should result.

Meanwhile Mary is a student observer at a local school; one of the teachers is her "monitor" responsible for arranging assignments for her and seeing that she is not overburdened. During the college months she will have participated in a few of the school activities mentioned above according to whatever practical arrangements can be made. Then, when her final examinations are over, she will be able to spend from six to eight weeks in the school on a full-time basis.

George Smith, another student, may decide to take a full B.A. course before becoming a teacher in either public or high school. The same process would apply to him. He may be required to take the special teachers' classes in at least five subjects. There will also be an opportunity for him to read in the history, philosophy, or psychology of education in connection with work he would be doing in at least one of these departments. He may also have not merely one, but from two to four years' association with a public school. As in the case of Mary, his teacher training is not a waste of time but a valuable help in his regular university studies. A further requirement is necessary at this level: he must achieve at least second class standing in his work.

Should George proceed to graduate study much the same pattern of work could be followed. He would fulfil the regular requirements of the faculty of graduate studies and the department concerned together with whatever study in teaching he may need or his department may require. Graduate departments can also make similar arrangements for teachers who wish to return for advanced work in the subjects they are teaching.

Still more apprenticeship can be arranged under professional auspices after the college work is completed and before final certification. I suggest that a year similar to the internship of the doctor should be required. Mary and George would then spend ten months, with salary, in different types of work divided appropriately among city, town, and rural schools, and among primary, intermediate, and senior classes. They would be apprentices to teachers and would observe, assist, and teach. The work they could do would be practical experience for them as well as much needed assistance in the schools. When this apprenticeship was completed the candidates, from whatever university level they came, could write the teaching profession's qualifying examinations. Their licence would then be issued by the *profession*, and it would set forth the subjects in which they qualified; the licence would ensure that each candidate knows what he is going to teach.

Under this arrangement prospective teachers would not be forced into the blind alley of the present programme in "education" which, because it is of no value in other fields and of generally low standing, discourages students from studying for the profession. More students will certainly be encouraged to qualify. The proposed scheme could assure them of an adequate background of liberal education together with practical experience of infinitely more use to them than existing

courses in "education." School authorities would find the programme of great assistance to them in the selection of teachers. They
would hire not just a teacher who has been certified with qualifications so vague that it is possible to put a physical training graduate
into the teaching of history, but a person whose preparation is
clearly set forth and who can be assigned properly to duties suitable
to his obvious qualifications.

The main check on the quality of the teacher would in this plan
be made at a natural point: while he is being trained and when he is
appointed. If care is taken then, the need for future interference with
him will be limited or removed. I have mentioned earlier that one of
the chief reasons for so much supervision of teachers at present is
carelessness in the training and appointing of teachers. If schools look
for the best they will get the best results. A second check on the
teacher would come from his own colleagues in the school and the
profession. With a truly professional association based on freedom
of activity, teachers will be united by more than mere financial
agitation; they will become interested in standards, and they will
soon develop for themselves levels of achievement and codes of
conduct impossible to ensure by outside regulation and inspection.
The third check on the teacher would be his own self-judgment.
Given a sense of responsibility, he will know he must do the job and
take the credit or blame himself. This stimulus is strong in any profession, and when it becomes a recognized and accepted force in
schools it will make teaching a satisfying challenge, encouraging the
able and stimulating the indifferent.

The professional organizations which a trust system permits will
replace the weak teachers' federations which today can give little real
leadership. Teachers will give them more support because professional loyalty will be directed towards the craft instead of a government office. For the same reason school authorities will seek their
advice and the public will respect their opinions. It is important that
teachers' federations be professional, that is, composed only of
teachers. The Canadian Education Association, now composed
largely of departmental officials, professors of "education," and the

like, would need to be disbanded with the disappearance of the administrators who today speak for education. There is, of course, nothing revolutionary in the type of professional organization being suggested; other professional bodies such as medical associations, bar associations, and engineering institutes are similarly organized, speak for their members, and represent them in a general way before both the authorities and the public.

Teachers' federations would participate in policy making through representation on the provincial Council of Education; in determining the standards of teacher training through co-operation with universities and schools and through the power to grant licences; and in the development of the profession through information services, research bureaus, publications, and the like, and through the leadership of distinguished teachers. It must be stressed again that the federations would not be trade unions, but professional associations: teachers' relationships with their employers would be personal; the main instrument for collective power and regulation would be the faculty of the individual school; salaries, hours, and working conditions would be for the schools and their staffs to decide; and professional regulations concerning these matters should be general and flexible. Like bar, medical, ecclesiastical, and trade associations, teachers' federations should respect the freedom of the individual members.

In the trust system, a school's relations with other schools would be largely a matter of association between staffs in a professional relationship. Nevertheless, like some universities and many schools now, it may not live up to its responsibilities to its pupils—a situation not unknown in institutions in other professions. Here the check would be professional rather than political. A practice similar to medical inspection of hospitals might be useful. The national teachers' organization would arrange a check of every school every three years by able leaders of the profession. A committee of three would visit "Central Memorial" under such an arrangement, discuss its curriculum, policies, and record with its staff, principal, and trustees, and advise and inform about standards prevailing elsewhere and expected by the profession. The committee's report could be made available to the faculty council and the board of trustees with obviously beneficial results to the school. Moreover, universities and employers who can refuse to recognize the graduates of inferior schools would be able to influence standards in a substantial way.

It must not be supposed that on adoption of this new system all will be professional sweetness and intellectual light. There will still be poor schools and weak teachers. I submit, however, that there will be far fewer poor schools and weak teachers than there are now because it will be harder to tolerate them than it is now. Consider what good schools and able teachers could do under a trust system unfettered by controls and unhindered by an average. Their leadership, non-existent today, would be a force similar to comparable leadership in business and professional life.

When I have discussed this plan with politicians and educationists their most serious criticism of it is that there are today too many schools and teachers who would not know what to do with freedom to teach if they had it. The truth of this observation is a sad commentary on the present system; it is certainly not a justification for continuing it. The trust principle cannot be applied to every school and teacher all at once, but at first only to the better schools (it is not hard to judge which they are) and to competent teachers. The others could be considered as branch offices and junior assistants until by improvement they deserved full confidence. The high turnover now operating in the profession would in itself ensure an influx soon of abler teachers trained under the new system. The profession would have to be reorganized; perhaps the new Canadian College of Teachers is already a step in that direction. Only properly qualified teachers should constitute it; the others would be regarded as apprentices, a status which they would enjoy in any other occupation. In this way the trust plan could be introduced gradually as conditions permitted.

Would not the effect of such a general reorganization in the schools in the end be both great and hopeful? Deadening, regulated routine for teachers could, I suggest, be replaced by individual and group initiative. Undignified kow-towing to powerful officials and dominating "experts" could give way to leadership by the profession itself and the gifted within it, and to proper consultation with true experts. The distant authority of the "department" would be displaced for the teacher by the authority of the school and of the profession. Teachers could become workers with souls, minds, and rights rather than minor civil servants moved like marionettes. Teaching could involve primarily the relations between individuals rather than the mechanical distribution of prescribed information under conditions of mass production. The school could become a community institution rather than a public utility, and it, together with its staff and its services, would enjoy the increased respect of pupils, parents, and taxpayers. Indeed, education itself should enter a new era of development simply because it would be freed from bondage.

The kind of curriculum, the methods of teaching, and the standards of achievement which should prevail in the individual schools are matters of great detail beyond the scope of this book. They are certainly not topics on which there has been or will be general agreement. I submit, however, that there would be more cooperation and agreement about them among those concerned under a trust system than there is at present. Teachers' federations would encourage adequate standards and they would have sufficient prestige to lead in the attainment of them. For the same reason teachers would pay more attention to their organizations, and, because they would be permitted some initiative of their own, they would keep abreast of professional developments. This type of leadership and *esprit de corps*, which no government office can provide, is encouraged from within in other professions and its effect on standards is obvious; similar arrangements in teaching are absolutely essential to the development of educational facilities and standards.

Once such arrangements are made, many of the weaknesses of the curriculum, teaching methods, and standards should disappear. The programme and the mechanics of operation would be based on the abilities of, and the relationships between, teachers and pupils, on the plain facts of employment, and on the demands of knowledge and training. Emphasis on mass-production, assembly line, and propaganda would be replaced by attention to human needs and professional skill. "Professional" would once again be associated with teaching and the worship of the official and the "expert" would decline.

Some of the elements of freedom would ultimately be extended to the pupils, although the school would, of course, exercise substantial control over them. As they grow older, the sense of responsibility pervading the school would influence them and encourage them to look more to their own efforts and expect less of those of others. The dull regulated routine and perpetual guidance which renders education tasteless, the "poor dear children" attitude which never permits pupils to be left alone to do anything by themselves, and "the state knows best" idea which is debilitating to young citizens in a democracy—all these would cease to be prominent features in the life of a school.

The examination system would need a drastic change if freedom of teaching is to be encouraged. Here again the state's influence must be removed. The mechanics involved would depend, of course, on the area concerned, but the control of examinations could be placed in the hands of the universities and the teaching profession. They know what pupils will be expected to do on leaving school, and they know what pupils have been doing in school. When the universities and the profession had been operating the examination system for some years, and after acceptable standards had been established in the schools, the system of accredited schools under which a school's own examinations are the basis of determining scholastic achievement might be revived. The universities and employers would then recognize the school's certificate as actual matriculation, the school would be relieved of the distracting burden of preparing for general examinations, and learning would be based on thinking rather than on the organized recital of the "right answers."

The promise of freedom for profession and individual raises the question of the democratic control of education which has been considered vital. Perhaps, some will fear, schools and teachers would become irresponsible, ignoring the public from which the funds to support them come. I submit that the public interest would be as safe in their hands as it is today in the hands of other professional institutions and workers and certainly far more certain to be wisely served than it is in the hands of a centralized governmental bureaucracy. Public opinion could never be ignored, and it, with professional opinion, would be sufficiently powerful to keep the people concerned responsible and active. They either do not operate in the public schools today, or are rendered ineffective because they are sifted through a political or departmental sieve. Under a school trust public opinion could be much more effectively expressed and, if necessary, controlled.

What, it will be asked, will guarantee that all pupils will get a basic minimum of education and that their opportunities will not vary too greatly from one area to another? In the first place I reject the idea that a centralized departmental authority and a standardized curriculum are guarantees of "education for all," for reasons stated in previous chapters. In the second place I submit that centralization and standardization as they are now encouraged are dangerous in education because they are far from being as "democratic" as they appear. Under a trust system there will still be a tendency towards provision of opportunity and uniformity, but this will be a more natural and inevitable one which is not artificially forced, and a more effective one because it is allowed to develop and grow with circumstances. Governments cannot turn on and distribute a regulated supply of education like electric energy. But schools organized on the basis of public ownership and individual enterprise can truly provide a high standard of education for all if given, not orders, but responsibility.

It has to be remembered, too, that there would be checks in this new system, all of which could be more flexible, yet stronger, than those which prevail today. In the training and licensing of teachers there would be the combined influence of the universities and the profession. In the hiring of teachers there would be recognized professional standards upon which the authorities of the schools could depend. In the determination of the curriculum there would be the combined ideas and efforts of those who must make it work in practice and the example set by other institutions and teachers. In the co-ordination of the efforts of different schools and teachers, there would be the influence of the universities and the professional associations. In the service to pupils there would be the opportunity and power to treat them as individuals rather than as statistics. In the service to the public there would be for safeguard the combined influence of the Council of Education, the professional organizations, the lay boards of trustees, the faculty councils, and the teachers: all of these will be more sympathetic with public opinion because they will be in closer touch with it and yet not subservient because they will have power to deal with it. Surely these groups and individuals should know more, do more, and be more responsible than a minister of education and other politicians, a hierarchy of superintendents and inspectors, and a host of pressure groups.

I state with great confidence that the public interest will be seen to be served as public respect for schools and teachers increases with their freedom. Indeed there would be greater public respect for and understanding of education itself. The starry-eyed expectancy of the zealous reformer, the narrow interest of the selfish group, and the penurious attitude of the "something-for-nothing" advocates, would, it is true, have much less scope because the teaching profession would be stronger to resist and because the power of the kind of political administration which is so dependent on votes would be diminished. Is this in any way to be regretted? On the positive side, public interest and public welfare would receive far more attention, because, bearing a new responsibility, schools and teachers would be able to remain in close, and yet fruitful, contact with them, and having done so, to prepare and carry out necessary proposals on their own. Democracy in the school system would be encouraged with the removal of all the superfluous middlemen who now stand between the schools and the people. At the end of his essay "On Liberty," John Stuart Mill wrote:

A government cannot have too much of the kind of activity which does not impede, but aids and stimulates, individual exertion and development. The mischief begins when, instead of calling forth the activity and powers of individuals and bodies, it substitutes its own activity for theirs; when, instead of informing, advising, and, upon occasion, denouncing, it makes them work in fetters, or bids them stand aside and does their work for them. The worth of a state, in the long run is the worth of the individuals composing it; and a state which postpones the interest of *their* mental expansion and elevation to a little more of administrative skill, or of that semblance of it which practice gives, in the details of business; a state which dwarfs its men, in order that they may be more docile instruments in its hands even for beneficial purposes—will find that with small men no great thing can really be accomplished; and that the perfection of machinery to which it has sacrificed everything will in the end avail it nothing, for want of the vital power which, in order that the machine might work more smoothly, it has preferred to banish.

The vital power is liberty; the means of developing it is trust; the place where it is needed most and where it will have the most beneficial effect on the entire democratic state is in the public schools.

Three questions immediately arise. Can the people stand a free educational system? Can teachers rise to the obligations which such a system will impose? Can pupils handle the responsibility which will be placed on them? If the answer is "no" to these questions, if dominance by the state is regarded as essential, then democracy is a sham. Democracy, however defined, presupposes a thinking, powerful people; in it there can be no playing down of human ability.

"Yes!" is *my* answer to these questions. The people will like, and thrive under, a free educational system, for they will find that it will serve them and not just cater to them. It is unfortunate that so many authorities feel they must pander to the lowest of public tastes, from those politicians who, to get votes, promise what they know to be wrong and hold back distasteful news, to those producers who entice with cheap premiums and hide the unripe with red cellophane. It is better in the long run to give the public the facts, fair, square, and often, for public tastes and judgment are sound when trusted, and the true interest of the public is far more important than the power of authorities or the sales of products. Education is too important a part of public welfare to be doled out to the people in glittering bargain packages of light easy-to-take preparations. The same people who will work hard for a living or fight hard for a cause will, if encouraged, rise to the challenge of the thirst for knowledge which is man's greatest appetite.

I would go so far as to say that teachers, if they cannot assume responsibility for the schools, should not be teaching. Children deserve better than untrained, subservient, often temporary hired help, which is how at least a third of those who teach now must be described. These would ultimately disappear with freedom of teaching, and others like them would be discouraged from entering the profession. The remainder are people with intelligence and character and the authority which refuses to give them the responsibility they merit and need deprives the country and its children of a fine type of leadership for the sake of its own power. A democratic country and its people need intellectual leadership just as much as political, economic, and military leadership, and it must come largely from teachers in the colleges and schools. When this fact is realized and recognized by means of freedom to teach, existing teachers will rise to the occasion and others will seek to exercise their talents by joining the profession.

Pupils also will rise to the challenge of a free system. They will have more respect for strong schools and teachers. They are more intelligent than older people think but most of them merely coast when there is too much regimentation. The limitless curiosity and ingenuity of pupils are best developed under genuine leadership. Training rather than stuffing, leading instead of managing, requiring rather than coaxing, trusting in place of herding are the techniques which education deserves and which children will appreciate. Young people will have to carry democracy into the future; they can do so only if they grow up under its auspices, understand its responsibilities, and appreciate its benefits. The place for them to start is in the schools.

Index

LANGUAGE, learning of, 115–19, 125
Lawyers, 18, 24, 42, 62, 84, 158
LaZerte, M. E., 30n, 41n, 92n, 104n
Leacock, Stephen, 122
Learned-Sills Report, 16
Legislature, 10, 11, 133, 148–9
Lewis, C. S., 113n
"Line" and "staff" functions, 31
Long, Marcus, 106n

MacCORKINDALE, H. N., 155n
MacIntosh, W. A., 44n
Macmillan, Prime Minister Harold, 58n
Maritime Provinces of Canada, 16
Mass media, 56, 63, 67, 72–4
Massey Commission, 95
Mathematics, teaching of, 94, 99, 102–3, 116, 126–7, 160
Meadows, S., 34n
Melbourne, Lord, 7
Merit rating, 83, 164
Methodology, 93–101
Mill, John Stuart, 24, 114, 180
Morgan, J. P., 150
Mowat, A. S., 65n
Munroe, D., 46n
Municipal government, see Government proposed trust system and, 138, 142–3

NEATBY, Hilda, 35
New Brunswick Teachers' College, 92, 93
Newman, Cardinal, 60
Normal schools, 29; description of, 90–5; government control of, 90; proposed abolition of, 165; see also teacher training
Nova Scotia, 104, 126

O'BRIEN, T., 135n, 136n
Officials, 5; curriculum and, 107–30, 129; dominance of, 27, 29–49, 86, 123, 129, 180; powers of, 29–42; proposed trust system and, 154–5; 165; public opinion and, 57–9, 77;

qualifications of, 42–9; schools and, 29–49, 59, 61, 64, 77
Ontario, 9, 104, 113–14, 126
Opposition, 5, 20
Orpen, Sir William, 120
Osler, Sir William, 121

PARKINSON'S LAW, 27, 109
Parties, political, 10, 73
Pedagogy, see "Education"
Penfield, Dr. Wilder, 115
Pitt, William, 120
Political interference, in business and professions, 6, 21; in education, 10, 12, 13, 14, 15, 16, 58, 59, 72, 76, 109
Politicians, 14, 16, 24, 59, 73, 77, 81, 84; business and, 133; dependence on administrators, 31; impatience with education 15, 77; interpretation of curriculum, 109–10
Pressure groups, 6, 10, 14; Minister of Education and, 19; schools and, 22, 24, 58, 62–6
Premier: cabinet appointments and, 17; Minister of Education and, 19; proposed Council of Education and, 141
Principal, school, 37, 51, 139, 162
Prior, L. J., 89n
Public opinion, 4, 5, 6, 7, 8, 22; control of, 130, 132; Minister of Education and, 19; schools and, 51–2, 58–66, 76, 81–2, 146–7, 148–9, 178–9; teachers and, 82
Public Works, 16, 39, 151; Department of, 151
Pupils, 25, 56; activities outside of school, 67–72, 114–15; capabilities of, 113–23; standards and, 95, 112; trust system and, 180–1

READING, 68–9
Roberts, G. L., 90n
Robson, W. A., 135, 149n, 150n